István Lukovich

Foil Fencing

Technique, Tactics, and Training
A Manual for Coaches and Coaching Candidates

SwordPlay Books

Published by SKA SwordPlay Books
www.swordplaybooks.com
3939 Victory Boulevard
Staten Island, NY 10314

Printed in USA

DEDICATED

*To the memory
of my unforgettable professor,
the late Dr. László Duronelly.*

István Lukovich

Contents

Rounded wall targets (See page 64)

Foreword

Fencing – since it is not only an individual sport, but also a sport of individuality – does not lend itself to the fixed definitions common to other sports. This is why it is difficult to write a book about it.

I have attempted to approach the sport from a practical point of view, make my text more readable, explain the terms in greater depth than usual, offer something to hold on to for those who are not versed in fencing's jargon, and to reveal a common denominator uniting the great fencers possessing an outstanding sense of form with the effective naturalists. While respecting the heritage of the classical methodology, I tried to face the challenges of *our own* period as well.

Acknowledging the fact that not even the best-edited book can show all the roles that the parts play in the whole, I have striven to shed light on the connections between its parts, touching upon the questions of the sport.

With this book, I pay homage to the great Hungarian coaches from whom I learned the profession, and who took me up, supported me, and taught me. To those fencers whose theoretical preparedness and practical work earned numerous gold medals for Hungarian fencing, I also dedicate this book and wish for my colleagues to benefit from its use.

The Author

I. Fencing: Profile and Characteristics

Fencing – the science of wielding the cutting and thrusting weapons – is a combat sport incorporating two genders (male and female) and three disciplines or weapon types: foil, saber, and epee. With a foil or epee, one can only thrust; with a saber, one can both cut and thrust.

The target area is smallest in foil and largest in epee. (From this point of view, saber stands in the middle.) According to the classical definition, foil is the weapon of technique, saber is the weapon of tactics, and epee is the weapon of tempo.

In foil fencing it is more difficult to follow the bouts, or to detect, understand, and differentiate the nuances of the actions. That is why it is more of a weapon for those who are amenable to its conventions. People with less fencing experience find it easier to follow the spectacular actions and plastic movements of the saber fencers. Epee is popular among its participants because of its combative spirit.

In all the disciplines, the opponents communicate with each other through footwork and actions with their weapons. Because the fencer's role varies between dictating the action and adjusting to the actions of his opponent, the fencer has to feel at home with both attack and defense, regardless of the fact that with time, one or the other role will become his strength.

The intellectual and physical battle manifests itself and becomes tangible in technique. The success of the attacks depends on dynamic space and time conditions: the existence, creation, harmonization, and utilization of speed, distance, and tempo.

Fencers with the most diverse abilities can all fight effectively. The majority of these abilities are tangible and measurable, tied to movement, while others are more abstract, complex, mental, and psychological.

Sometimes more, other times fewer conditions are needed for scoring a touch. The scale is wider than in some other sports, i.e. athletics or swimming. The variously related abilities can help each other out in case of need. This would be unimaginable in, for example, the 100 meter sprint, since physical speed is the sole and irreplaceable ingredient of a successful performance.

The combatants bring their personal characteristics into their bouts.

Outsiders are put off by some of these characteristics until they become unaccustomed to the sport's specific atmosphere and its inner world. Some of the hardest for outsiders to endure indeed seem negative to ordinary common sense, but these can become profitable virtues on the fencing strip. A fencer cannot win without being able to act, to deceive or even to "scam" the opponent. A good fencer is like a good actor, who can play any role from comedy to drama.

The most important fencing abilities are like the colors spread around a painter's palette. The factors that shape the results depend on the situation. They are individual and unique. The fencer's best capabilities outline his character, determine his style, and influence his effectiveness.

Sight is the main faculty for gathering information. The guidelines received through the fencer's *touch* and *hearing* serve only as supplements. One cannot count on blade contact when it comes to saber, due to the nature of the weapon. On the other hand, it is easier to follow saber actions; the foil and epee blades, moving on a plane, are more difficult to follow, especially in the case of complex bouts.

Elements that can be taught, virtues that can be refined, specifics of the sport, moral, mental, and psychological characteristics all play a role in the developmental system of fencing. Their cooperation or collision result from the fencer's momentary wants and needs and the dialectic based on the opponent's intentions; they are partly based on chance and partly on the demands of the bout. Their complex connections can be illustrated in three dimensions. The changes of cadence and rhythm could be written out in a musical score.

As of now, sport science still owes us an in-depth examination of all the components of fencing and their practical consequences. To isolate only a few abilities, to make a fetish of them, to favor them, to evaluate them in an unsophisticated way can lead to false conclusions and fatal and extreme oversimplification. A casual observer might conclude that the abilities required for fencing work together much more easily than they actually do in real life. That is why we must focus on the *interactions* of fencing abilities, not the abilities in isolation. Therefore, since sport science will not be able to deal with the interaction of fencing abilities in the near future, we have to be satisfied with the deductions resulting from practical experiences.

As with other sports, we use general terms in fencing to name the abilities. Because of this, we necessarily commit the mistake of generalizing, which can be deceptive. The observer will be susceptible to identifying i.e. the speed of a sprinter with the speed of a fencer or the flexibility of a high-jumper with the flexibility of a fencer's legs.

The electric signaling machine has replaced the four side judges, who were often unreliable. However, the work of the referee, whose decisions are based on the conventions like priority ("right of way"), still entails the possibility of errors, especially when it comes to borderline cases. Fencers can try to compensate for this by attempting to strive for articulate fencing. (In epee fencing, the referee has the easiest job.)

Coaches rarely influence the fencer's choice of weapons. If they happen to be asked for advice, they should advise epee for taller people and ones who lack a feeling for conventions (right of way). The importance of height is not so significant in foil and saber.

One can only live, feel, and identify in an experienced way with the events happening on the strip, if one is something of an insider. This is one of the special features of fencing. The size of the audience is thus much smaller compared to other sports that offer spectacular and comprehensible action right from the beginning. However, here in Hungary, at least, public opinion looks forward to big fencing competitions like the World Championships and the Olympics. Besides rooting for the best fencers, they also expect good results.

Although sometimes new nations join the circulation of the fencing world, the fencing population of a given nation does not change rapidly over time. Competing in numbers with other sports would be impossible. Any forced attempt to increase the numbers of participants, the attempt to increase the head count has always failed due to a simple fact: no amount of parental pressure can replace the inner impulse necessary for undertaking and accepting the sport. Body building drugs or stimulants have little to do with fencing. The size of the muscles does not shape the results. The effects of doping are unpredictable, even in one-day competitions, though they cannot be disregarded during the breaks between bouts and rounds. In fencing, then, it is still possible to compete with one's "natural" abilities – as long as we disregard the development that comes through training.

Fencing is also unique because of the interaction between the fencer and the fencing master and the need for individual lessons.

Regardless of the tendencies of this modern age and the development of technology, to be a coach in our sport still remains a profession rather than a job. The specifics, the burdens, the requirements, the uniquely tedious quality of the work – and at the same time, its beauties – can only be understood and felt by someone who himself has taught. The hierarchy of coaching consists of a base of hard-working coaches who copy the work of their colleagues and, above them, the coaches with outstanding talents whose work is worth copying. These top-ranked coaches, even if they do not create a lasting school, will definitely become examples that prove the written and unwritten rules of pedagogy and psychology. The best become milestones in the history of fencing because of their philosophy, their enviable physical skills, and their suggestive individuality.

Fencing masters must sometimes be armorers, leaders of sport club sections, storekeepers, and administrators, all in one person. In small provincial clubs, during study circles in schools, the coaches are required to perform all of the duties of Physical Education teachers.

Fencing is one of Hungary's most successful sports. Besides our traditional weapon, the saber, we are part of the world's elite in all the weapon types today.

Many people ask whether fencing has a future. Will the people of the future have time and the energy to be absorbed in a sport that requires years to learn and to ripen? Will our changing age and the rapid rhythms of life ruin fencing's chances? Will it become an obsolete anachronism? Will it be able to keep its place in the midst of the booming development of technology and the numerous new sports waiting to rush in and take its place?

Contrary to some expectations, interest in fencing has not decreased. There is a growing head count sufficient to pass it on, regardless of age and fashion. As in the past, it is evident that there will be people in the future who will wish to test their abilities on the strips. Besides being fun, fencing is a challenging sport that shapes a person's character when it is done competitively, allowing the person to prove his complex self.

The components of the fight and their roles. The necessary ingredients for successful performance: their nature, study, scope, and tasks.

The abilities required for scoring touches are complex and interwoven, varied in use, differing in emphasis, and deployed in differing ratios. There can be no absolute order of importance among them. First and foremost, however, the fencer relates to the distance. In order to achieve his goals, he maneuvers on the strip, combining half-steps, whole steps, jumps, slides and sudden stops, striving for unpredictable changes in direction, cadence and rhythm.

Sense of distance

The sense of distance requires judging the distance separating the opponents. When it operates properly, it signals changes of distance with the speed and precision of a computer. Live battles, bouts for stakes, experience, and long years of training are behind such a heightened sense.

The fencer calibrates the distance based on the height of the body and the length of the limbs (in the case of child fencers, this can only happen once physical development is finished). He also judges his opponents with the same parameters. The distance to be crossed depends, more or less, on physical speed.

The movements of the weapon and the footwork have to be coordinated with the intended action in light of each weapon's traits and rules. Distance modifies the hand-foot coordination, the position of the beats, binds, parries, and whether they are executed closer to or farther from the body, made steeper or flatter, and the progressivity of feint attacks and feint ripostes.

The opponents can face each other at short, medium, or long distance, or at infighting distance. Short distance is measured by about the length of an extended arm, medium distance by the lunge, and long distance by the length of a direct thrust with a step-forward lunge, balestra, or fleche.

Close combat (infighting) happens at a distance closer than that of the extended arm. (This forces the greatest changes in technique. Even though lessons are given using standard distances, during a bout the fencer has to adapt his footwork and flexible weapon handling to small fractions of distances.)

Technique

Technique, which is born out of specific norms and for special aims, is the sport's formal side, the part that can be followed and acquired most easily. It can be developed to a high degree. (In its counterpart, tactics, natural abilities are generally decisive.) The tools of technique are made up of basic solutions and their variations and combinations. Technique can be divided into three parts. The first part consists of the practical actions used in live fencing; the second is made up of actions taught in order to develop abilities and skills (for example, semicircular and circular transfers are the best exercises leading up to semicircular and circular parries); while the third part consists of those curiosities and rare exceptions that nowadays only tend to exist in theory – for example, the quarte (or, in the case of opposite-handed fencers, the sixte) flank single circular feint of a bind side thrust that evades the opponent's ceding parries.) The line separating the curiosities from the routine actions changes as fencing styles change with the times.

Actions with the weapons, directly, or with footwork, indirectly, threaten the opponent. The possibility of partnership among the simple plots spreads out the repertoire that can be taught on a large scale.

The fencer's stance assures the ability to start, his footwork assures mobility, and his hand technique assures the possibility of touches and the defense with the weapon. Shaping these into skills requires large amounts of work. The standard that can be reached is determined by the nature of each skill, the fencer's ability to coordinate the movements, the form, the cadence, the sense of rhythm, patience, and desire.

Technique, even if it is not the sole requirement of success, is certainly a major factor of efficiency, due to the advantages that result from the effective handling of the weapon. Not even the naturalist tendencies of the present day can call into question the main technical virtues of many competitors. The almost undetectable movement of the point that launches the attack, the progressive movements of the blade, the perfect concert of the hands and the feet, the execution of the actions based on the principle of the shortest way, the use of circumferential velocity – these are all arguments that support the statement above. The use of circumferential velocity appears, for example, in foil, when a seconde parry is followed by a thrust thrown to the opponent's back. A person depending on his technical development in a bout cannot allow such a large liberality, i.e. the wider than necessary movements, which are reserved for someone with much better physical capabilities.

Dealing with technique in its proper place is crucial for the sport's essence, aesthetic, authenticity, and appeal. (Sloppy technique depreciates the sport and leads it into a dead end. The imperfect leading of the blade and the unsure point can wreck even the best idea.) Practicing technique is the center of gravity of the coach's work. The coach can do the most for his students in this field.

Instinctive motor habits have to be fought when learning technique. The student must quit starting with the foot, get over the sudden, instinct-like reactions, and give up following the opponent's blade, while in every situation, using the shortest ways and the shortest methods.

The fencer has to become accustomed to starting with the point, since due to its weight, it is the part of the weapon that can be mobilized the fastest; he must master the narrow amplitudes, disengages, binds, beats, the work of the fingers, wrist, and forearm that proportionately help each other out when parrying.

It is easier to teach the plastic movement of saber technique in space, compared to the narrower spatial field of the thrusting weapons. With a few cuts that go haywire, we at best "knight" our partner. The side cut can hit right under the opponents armpit or just above the waist. In saber, the hit remains a hit, no matter what, while this type of inaccuracy usually results in a passé in foil and epee. In epee, we tend to give points instead of areas as targets. For these – using a shooting metaphor – one has to "hit the bull's-eye" in a series, for the point to hit steadily in a bout.

Actions can be best familiarized with medium paced technical work, while at the same time forming a muscle structure suited to the sport. Forcing speed ahead of time can lead to false motor habits. Even though speed is part of a successful action, it should not be forced as long as technique does not present an acceptable picture. Trying too hard can ruin the order of the muscles involved in the action, as well as involve the use of muscles that are not required at all. So if the student commits mistakes, the speed should be reduced first. If this does not help, that is when you have to turn to other tools.

The attacking and defending actions have to be taught in the proper order and proportion according to the weapon's traits and requirements. The combined actions and solutions with more steps have to be taught in proportion to the individual's skills.

Foil fencers usually prefer attacks, while epee fencers usually prefer counterattacks. In both weapons, actions in the high lines are more frequent, but those in the lower line cannot be left out of the bouts or the lessons. Practicing them leads to the development of actions; using them increases their range while diversifying them.

The parry plays the main role in a foil fencer's defense. Counterattacks are secondary. In epee, the point is the main defense line. In foil, the parry is followed by the one- and then the two-cadence parry-ripostes.

Although technique can be taught to a group, the individual lesson is the special stage for teaching it in all its aspects (time, content, methods, and intensity.) In the lesson, the

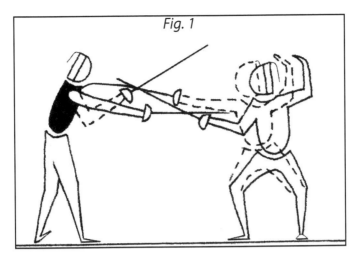

Fig. 1

coach, using the reciprocal of the student's action, plays the role of the teacher, partner, and opponent. That is, he is both the active agent of the work, but also, because he is repeatedly hit, the "suffering subject" as well (Fig. 1). Other sports have similar training methods, but the individual lesson is never so dominant, consistent, characteristic – and tiring – as in fencing. Since a great deal depends on his contribution, no coach has the luxury of giving a lesson without practical knowledge of the technique.

Lessons are not only a part of teaching technique; they are also part of maintaining it. Well-trained competitors use lessons with their coaches mainly or solely for this.

One cannot expect the techniques of a lesson to properly and fully appear in live fencing. Too much excitement, due to the stakes, will distort technique, while the student's capability to replicate the lesson is diminished. Finally, it is also impossible to go through all of the possible formulas during the lessons. In sudden situations, a fencer has to improvise based on the learned material. This is connected to the students' elastic ability to adapt. Even though students may be similar to each other in their technical level (the difference in the level of tactics may be greater for people who are on the same level in technique), the striving for development does not bring the same results for everyone. After reaching

17

the fencer's maximum, we can only talk of maintaining the technique. The mistakes that cannot be eliminated will stick to the fencers' movements, like a sort of stylistic mark.

Regardless of the strong differences in the rules, there are many similarities in the techniques of foil and epee. Based on this ground, foil, fenced with the lighter weapon, can be understood as a preparatory tool for epee. Nowadays, however, it is usual that even children begin fencing with the weapons they will compete with later on. This is possible today, since the fencing manufacturers produce special weapons for them as well.

The sense of the blade is an essential characteristic of cutting and thrusting weapons. The ability to come to know, to be familiar with, to become accustomed to, and to be able to use the weapon's physical traits and behavior, allows the fencer to approach the foil, epee, and saber in the language of fencing. The weapon functions in proportion to the constant sense of the blade.

The necessary amplitude of the movements, the function of the edge, the back, the point, the forte of the blade, the middle part, the weak part – all these become embodied in the security of hitting, becoming a tangible thing. Be it a beginner, an advanced, or a competitive fencer, the technical work conditions this skill as well.

Technique had the utmost importance in the era of dry foil fencing. With only a small exaggeration, we could say that the most important requirement was finely chiseled technique. This gave elegance to the fencers of that period. Today, other abilities have come closer and closer to technique in importance. The *pace* has become faster. It is necessary to recruit fencers who are fast in a continuous series of movements, not only lunges and fleches from immobility, and whose speed over distance and ability to accelerate is matched by their ability to stop rapidly and to switch directions.

Since the proportion of fast and slow fibers in an individual is coded from birth, it must be noted that fencers with predominantly slow fibers cannot be sculpted into quick-footed competitors, not even with the most sophisticated methods. They have to be switched to epee. A relatively slow foot is not a tragedy there. Epee, this weapon often waiting for the right moment to be used, allows a number of not too fast fencers to prevail.

Nevertheless, because in fencing, unlike many other sports, it is possible to make other abilities compensate for a deficiency in one of them, a number of relatively slower fencers can become quite proficient. These have to be investigated and developed individually. Many people can compensate for their deficiency in speed with a heightened sense of tempo, a steady point, good nerves, patience, and finally, the ability to penetrate the opponent's thoughts – seeing, anticipating, imitating, preventing, or reacting to his thoughts and intentions ahead of time.

Footwork

In rapid footwork, the mobility of the foot and the ankle matter more than that of the whole leg. Setting the feet down quickly and picking them up quickly are especially decisive when it comes to series made up of narrow amplitudes and small steps. Quickening and slowing the pace and changing the range of speeds are as important as absolute speed.

There was a time when the speed of the fencer's legs was compared to the sprinter's, and coaches tried to develop it with methods found in athletics. In time, however, they discovered that there is only a hypothetical connection between the two types of speed. (If there had been a real connection, the problem of physical speed could be solved by recruiting unused sprinters.) A coach should not make his beginners run (this helps nothing when it comes to competitors) except over a short distance, connected with starts on 20-30 meters at the most, during the period when physical conditioning happens after the dull season.

Besides physical factors, other things can influence the speed of the hands and the arms. The speed of the flicked (thrown) thrusts and cuts is the result of circumferential velocity. Also important are the amplitude, the progressivity, the order of the parts or portions, their sequence, beginning with the edge or the point, and the execution of the technique along the shortest possible distance from the launching until the end of the action.

Strength

As the principal component of the physical work of fencing, footwork is what first and foremost requires the raw presence, and spectacular cooperation of *strength*. (The foot is the main weight carrier. The hand and the arm have only to move the weapon, which is much lighter than the body.) The lower limbs are expressively strong; the muscles are characteristically hypertrophied. The muscles' shapes illustrate the varying load (function) placed on the legs. This fact is worth keeping in sight during dedicated strength development.

We cannot find a similar requirement for strength when it comes to the hands and the arms. Although there are differences between the various weapons (e.g., saber uses the muscles of the forearm more extensively, which can be verified by foil fencers switching to saber), anything that happens under the name of strength here, is generally due to the fingers behind the guard (the strength of the weapon hand and the fingers are proven by research) and the way they apply the laws of physics. Leverage (mechanical advantage) dominates in the case of parries, beats, binds, when lifting the parry, binds in seconde, transfers, bind thrusts, bind side thrusts. With saber parries, the edge of the fencer's blade faces the edge of the opponent's. This position can defend against even the strongest cuts with minimal use of strength, while the fencer uses only his thumb, index finger, and fifth finger.

It is unnecessary to develop additional strength in order for thrusts to exceed the necessary 500 grams in foil and 750 grams in epee. Whatever strength is needed can be attained through the practice of technique. It is more important to develop the muscles of the torso. Fencing itself will not lead to this, and during the bout, the muscles of the back have a huge role in supporting the fencer's posture.

A number of similar exercises are at our disposal to work the lower limbs. In this sense, the repertoire for developing the muscles of the hands and the arms is quite poor.

Endurance

Fencing competitions consist of a series of bouts that alternate with longer or shorter breaks. The fencers have to produce larger achievements under grave physical and situational pressure, while the mental and nervous demands continuously increase as the fencer becomes more tired.

The pounding pace of the bouts must be maintained over a long term; the fighting spirit must be both maintained and inspired, even after multiple unavoidable setbacks. The interruptions have to be pulled through so the spirit will not break and the reflexes will stay sharp. The coach must prepare the fencer for these special demands during supplementary training that is spiced up with occasional changes of pace, even though the professional work remains the same.

Endurance is a complex entity, a special product that speaks for itself. It only becomes whole through the harmonious cooperation with the mental-physical side. Any disturbance of the desired balance can be at the expense of success. It is difficult, if not impossible, to find parallels for it in the movements of other sports in order to develop, maintain, or enhance it.

Fencers' short-term endurance can be measured by fencing a bout, mid-term endurance by fencing a round, and long-term endurance by fencing a competition.

If we want to develop endurance through running, we should take into consideration to following:

- Fencing is not "long-distance running," so do not make the distance too long;
- Avoid running the distance at a continuous

speed (fencers do not need the endurance developed by steady running). Apply changes in the pace, and, *"horribile dictu,"* total rests as well. For these rests, the fencers should stop totally, just as they do for a shorter or longer period at the end of a bout, and only after this should they speed up again;

- Running is not a goal, only a tool. It can be replaced by games. Basketball, or five-man and/or indoor soccer, popular among fencers, regardless of the danger of getting injured, may even be more useful than running, because here there are opponents, situations that have to be solved, and a tool that has to be handled. The game is similar to fencing in many regards, but at the same time it is a tool to relax the athlete's nervous system, because of the different emotional connections, for the person who is overloaded with his own sport.

Sense of tempo

The time appropriate for action is called the *tempo* in fencing. This can have physical or mental origins and nature. Since an opponent caught in a tempo is partially or totally incapacitated, the touch resulting from a tempo has a greater psychological effect.

The physical occasions for tempos have tangible signs; the psychological occasions have signs that can only be inferred. That is why it is more difficult to catch a psychological tempo. (Intuition, feelings, and foresight can help a lot in this.)

Tempo can be served by:
- The footwork
- The phase of an activity with the weapon
- Any influence affecting attention, such as distraction, the fluctuation of focus, absence of attentiveness, or fatigue

The physical occasions for tempos are based on the simple fact that the moves and movements we begin cannot be stopped in time, and our newer movements cannot be launched in time as new signals appear. If a fencer launches an attack, he will be vulnerable while he is in motion and might not be able to react in time to the signals that give hints about his opponent's intentions.

Some physical cues for a tempo are:

- A noticeable start
- A wider movement than required or intended
- A shift in position
- An uncontrollable reflex-like movement
- A parry signaling a false attack
- A false signal
- Beats, binds, or changes recognized in time, ones that can be followed with the naked eye
- Slow, lazy, long advances
- Movements repeated mechanically or predictably

These cues have to be imitated symbolically during the lessons. In the beginning, the coach should mimic with obvious and large movements, so the fencer would not only start in a tempo, but finish in it as well (Fig. 2). The length of the tempo should be decreased gradually, advancing towards a realistic amplitude (Fig. 3). The timing of the correct tempo

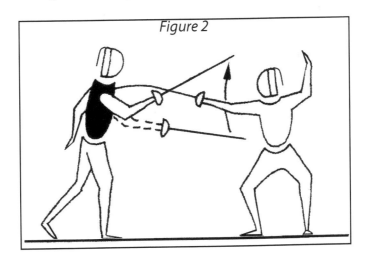

Figure 2

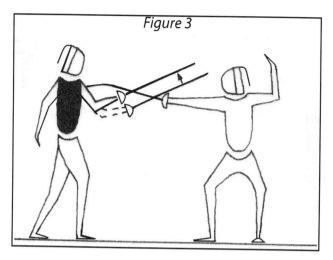

Figure 3

should be changed in the end, so the student is pressured to choose the time that best suits him.

The reason for the appearance of a psychological tempo can be searched for in the nature of attention; the varying amplitudes of its sine waves give psychological tempos. No matter how much we want to, we cannot always pay attention to everything. Our attention, like our body, becomes fatigued. Even the most persistent attention fluctuates. During the waning stage and at the bottom we are relatively incompetent; our reaction becomes more difficult, late, and sometimes, if the tempo is too big, we might even not be able to react at all. (The partner strives to play for this with series of actions that attempt to put the opponent to sleep, with moves that distract the attention, or with idle patience.)

The symptoms of psychological tempo – the waning of an opponent's attention, distraction, fatigue, lack of concentration – cannot be artificially recreated in the lesson; therefore such tempo types can only be studied during bouts.

Long-lasting tempos are rare; they usually appear in the movements of beginners. In order to exploit momentary tempos, a fencer needs quick reaction time, physical speed, intuition, foresight, the ability to judge one's chances of success. There are instances when the faintest signals have to be used to deduce the moment for a tempo. People "born" with a sense of tempo are usually the only ones who can do this.

Even if unintentionally, a fencer's actions are accompanied by breaks, stalemates, delays between phases, and lack of attention. That is why all of us are open to the dangers of unintentional tempo possibilities. If our opponent exploits these opportunities and plays on the game of tempo, his chances will be better than if he only tried to take advantage of our tactical or technical errors. A good fencer not only searches for such occasions, he tries to create them according to his intentions and knowledge, steering his partners into situations that benefit him.

It is the task of the lessons to accustom the student to the tempo. However, only when the student no longer needs to concentrate 100% on technique can the lesson move on to teach him how to start an action at a suitable time.

Tactics

Tactics have a major role in determining the outcome of the bout. Among people with similar levels of technique, tactical ability is what separates the competitors from the recreational fencers.

Tactics is the sum of a reflex-like way of judging the situation, deciding regarding it, and acting on it; it is the mental side of a bout, the ability to know how to win. It is the chance, possibility, and at the same time the compulsion for the fencer who is forced to fence the bout. It allows the fencer who has the tools of knowledge to think rationally, act precisely, and perform successfully. (Tactical ability is able to compensate for technical incapability in a number of regards, thus lifting fencing to the rank of an improvisational activity.) Its moral and mental catalysts are characteristic of the individual in everyday life as well. It is impossible to fight without courage, faith, and confidence. People whose hands shake in high-stakes moments, who are afraid that their idea will fail, usually leave the strip as losers.

Tactics is the manifestation of intentions applied to beat the opponent. It is the essence of the sport, a crucial part that is hidden and takes places behind the scenes. It is the execution of a decision based on the judgment of the power relations and the use of mediating tools; that is, the mobilization of skills and abilities to achieve success. Complicated chains of thought often take the form of the simplest actions in practice. This is more or less why laymen cannot really follow the events happening on the strip. This part of the sport is a closed world. Outsiders usually hear only afterward about the hidden springs of action. Fencers play chess in their minds. They try to find out each other's thoughts and intentions; they try to process, prevent, counteract, or surpass those thoughts.

The possibilities of tactics move in a wide range from a mild psychological stirring to effective activities with the weapon. Usually we witness the most plausible solutions. Unusual solutions tend to be the right of the most talented fencers. The phrase "the exception that proves the rule" often happens the other way around in tactics. Sometimes the most hair-raising things succeed because no one expects them to happen.

Since not even the greatest tactician can consider every possibility – not even a computer could make such quick and exhaustive calculations in real time – one has to rely on the most plausible solutions while striving to win. One must risk the action with the highest probability of success. The thought inspiring the tactics has to be made up while underway.

One cannot cling rigidly to a tactical plan prepared off the strip before the bout. (Elastic adaptation is an important part of tactics.) The person beaten the previous day can appear with new thoughts the next. Loss usually awaits those who cannot change.

Tactics can be built on the fencer's own virtues or on the opponent's weaknesses. A good fencer counts on both possibilities.

A fencer can step up as an initiator or an acceptor. Due to the changes in the roles (active, passive, adapting, or dictating), the bout shows a wavering image; calmer and more vehement periods succeed each other irregularly.

The actions required by the realities of probing, reconnaissance, and preparation are validated by the touch.

Everyone replies to the questions posed by the opponent in their own way. It is difficult, if not impossible, to give highly effective answers without "getting inside the bodies" of one's opponents. A born tactician has a rich imagination, is full of ideas, tasks, risks, and his faith in success is undiminished. He improvises, selects, decides, and acts based on his reflexes.

A fencer should be careful with advice coming from the coach. Often, a fencer does not know what to do with such advice, and he would achieve more on his own. Each fencer is unique when it comes to *how, how much,* and *how in-depth* that fencer can receive advice in case of need. Fencers – who serve as both privates and commanding generals on the strip – have to make their own decisions.

Beginners cannot be confronted with the questions of tactics too early. The coaches have to wait until the beginners gain a solid knowledge of technique. But tactics offers the users a simple, yet more colorful, diversified use of solutions for a flat technique.

Can tactical ability be taught?

A majority within the profession stand up for teaching tactics and the possibility of teaching tactics. They incorporate typical behavior forms into their lessons. Empathy and authentic assistance is needed for these to appear.

Skeptics view tactics as a theoretical study and that is how they teach it. Their work in this field relies on giving pieces of advice, hints, or illustrating the alternatives to a chosen action. They leave the execution up to the students. These skeptics compare an aptitude for tactics to a gift for drawing or for business, for a writer's imagination or a talent for music. That is to say, they view it as a gift that can be shaped from the outside only minimally or not at all. They believe that it is an absurdity to develop, substitute, and cultivate such ability in students who totally lack or have only a small tendency for it. Thus, only the forms of action that appear in stereotyped situations can be taught. A born tactician figures these out on his own, and learning the stereotypes is not enough for someone to become a talented fencer. The question is whether it is worth teaching tactics to those who have less ability in this department.

It is true that one can add less to the foundations of tactical ability in the name of learning or gathering experience, than one can in the realm of technique. Nevertheless, tactics can be, should be, and must be taught. The field for practicing tactics is the "silent lesson," the lesson with variations and combinations. These lessons are where fencers learn how to think and act in patterns.

Thanks to tactics, fencing is accompanied by great nervous strain. By the end of the season, a fencer wears out, psychologically rather than physically. Tangible signs for this are apathy, indifference, and competing without spirit. That is why the length of the season and the number of important competitions must be determined carefully. The off-season, longer than in other sports, should be turned to replenishing the nerve system and the psyche.

The traits for fencing go hand in hand, branch off from a number of intersections, with numerous overlaps serving success based on a complicated hierarchy.

All the abilities have to be on standby; they have to be mobilized, put to action, or extracted without delay. Constant readiness goes together with nervous tension. Success depends on small fractions of the moment.

The line of actual abilities changes in every situation. The main points and the proportions change as well. Characteristics that play a leading role at one moment become walk-ons at another or must wait in the wings for their turn. The relationship of the abilities fluctuates constantly – now dependent, now superordinate, now coordinate.

Ingredients for fencing success

It is not possible to offer a recipe, a proportion, and a dose for the prescription for fencing success, since science still owes us the means to measure the most important characteristics. Creating harmony between the conflicting factors is the method of bringing out the maximum from everyone.

All of the abilities have to be developed equally in the beginning, but when a fencer's most prominent talents begin to show, they have to be prioritized. Without forgetting the necessary maintenance of weaker abilities that cannot develop any further (these should be put at the service of the dominant abilities as a kind of side dish), we should strive to develop the individual's most characteristic abilities.

The road to becoming a competitor is long, bumpy, full of pitfalls, and also influenced to a high degree by luck. The results cannot be foreseen. Sometimes the desired results appear on schedule; in other instances there can be fencers who have to wait much longer to achieve the results they are fighting for. This certifies the phrase: talent, to a very great extent, is the result of perseverance.

Sports science has not yet answered the question of criteria for fencing: that is, to enumerate the prerequisite skills that would enable us to select winning fencers in advance. The reason for this is the sport's subtle nature (you cannot pick only one ability to reach the goal), the differing nature of the abilities, and the fact that the usable related branches of knowledge and their neighboring sciences have yet to provide us with traits that could be used as starting points or proof in fencing. As long as nothing happens in this field, the sport itself will choose the people who are fit for it, and the talented will choose themselves.

Fencing can be successfully pursued for a long time. (That is why it is not worth starting it too early.) Top competitors often reach the peak period of their results when they are over thirty. Generally, a competitor with a sound routine is able to replace the physical abilities used up by the years with calm judgment, courageous risk taking, and a pinpoint sense of distance. Although physical capabilities are in the foreground nowadays, they cannot be the sole conditions and single trustees of success. A fencer becomes smarter over time. He is able to use his virtues and mistakes in a favorable way. Tactics is timeless; its moral, mental, and psychic catalysts survive the physical ones.

At what age should fencing instruction begin? What should be the goals and methods of youth instruction?

Although the nature of the sport contradicts the mental and physical characteristics of youth, we systematically coach children as young as 7-8 years old. Supporters of the idea, to start training at an early age, base their reasons on two things:

1. An early start counteracts the attraction of sports that are more popular, more glamorous, or easier to master.

2. Those who start earlier gain such an advantage that latecomers will probably not be able to catch up and become discouraged.

So far, experience seems to contradict these arguments.

Many early starters say goodbye to fencing early. Often only two or three children remain out of a group of fifteen or twenty. Fencers, competitors will not suffer any disadvantages if they learn the sport later, as the careers of some great fencers show.

Why some young fencers leave early

1. The reality of fencing is very different from the sword-fighting that the child imagines.

2. The strict technical discipline pushes young fencers away. Often they make the decision almost at the very beginning, when another sport can offer more tangible results with less of an investment.

3. The lack of adaptation of methods used in teaching adults. (In order to train youths, a person needs to identify better with their age, needs more imagination, more empathy, and more moderation, than

when working with older groups or adults.)

4. The psychological trauma of defeat that is more difficult for a younger person to cope with than for an adult.

The best coach for youth fencers

1. Places multi-faceted training ahead of early specialization, creating a solid base for studying fencing as if it were a higher level of mathematics. (The vain hope that omitting a solid base will give advantages to the beginner has led to numerous disappointments.) Everything that – for a competitive fencer – is only a supplement to the training, an additional element, and a recreation – must be the main aspect, the backbone of training for children.

2. Bases all his methods – his pedagogy, his expectations, his exercises, the topics, length, and intensity of the training sessions – on the group's anatomical, physiological, and psychological nature, when it comes to planning, organizing, and performing the trainings. Allowing for a game at the end of the training session results in satisfying the exercising needs of the children based on their own imagination.

3. Uses his energy to make the children like fencing, instead of using it to prepare them for premature competitions.

4. And finally, waits patiently for the best time for beginning: waits for the child in question to try other sports also, gain experience, and only commit himself to fencing later on, based on his own decision. The likelihood of staying in fencing is greater this way, compared to a child who starts without any antecedent.

.

II. The Coach's Work: Its Special Qualities

Fencing cannot be learned without a coach. It cannot be self-taught. Some sports can be learned this way, but not fencing. Even in those sports, outside guidance is necessary.

The coach's work is complex. The next generation of fencers must be recruited. The recruits have to be trained. Groups have to be set up according to ages. Training exercises have to be connected and their execution must be checked. The education of the group must be directed. Mistakes have to be corrected. The students who face the mirrors and targets have to be assigned activities to proceed with. Lessons have to be given. Paired exercises have to be set up. Competitions have to be organized and run and students have to be escorted to them. In case of necessity, the roles of the armorer have to be fulfilled as well.

The cphysical strain on the coach is at its maximum when giving lessons. In other sports, verbal instruction is the coach's main medium. Swim or sprint or kayak coaches do not swim, run, or paddle with their students; basketball, soccer, and handball coaches rarely partner their students on the court. In fencing, however, the dominant coaching activity is moving with the students, weapon in hand. (The intensity and length of the lesson is connected to the coach's age and strength.) If we reflect that mistakes have to be continuously corrected, with methods according to the changing circumstances; that various students succeed each other, slow, fast, beginner, advanced, clumsy, talented; that the work takes place in a tight and loud fencing hall; that the last lesson of the day must be approximately the same quality as the first one; then it becomes evident that the profession is one where coaches are under a lot of psychological, as well as physical strain. That is why the coach must strive to keep himself in good physical and mental condition.

A fencer wants to take lessons from a coach he trusts. This is so fundamental that it cannot be ignored by anyone who wants to succeed. Students are generally assigned to coaches, but if the student has the opportunity to select the coach, he will weigh two factors: professionalism and personality. For young beginners, the coach's age (so that the student can identify with the coach) and pedagogical style are also very important. Professional qualifications generally influence the decisions only of advanced and competitive fencers.

The coach should keep up with the newest discoveries of related sciences. He should master the technique and tactics of all three weapons and know the strength requirements of each. He should be able to give blade for the most complex actions as well. He should have automated coaching movements. He should be flexible, with a receptive nature, always striving for more, for something better, willing to train himself. An unwavering ambition should burn in him and drive him forward for newer and newer results. From the start, he should have only an open mind. He should be able to objectively judge the things he observes in others.

The coach should shape his students to be ambitious, to strive for and succeed in reaching higher goals, even if they have to expect fatigue and sacrifices. His love for his profession should be felt in his work. He should teach happily and with joy, even when he is tired and full of problems. He should make himself find happiness during such occasions as well.

The coach's guidance should be worth following, related to general human behavior and connected to coaching and competing. He should keep his cool even during tense and heated competitions. With the use of his self-control and willpower he should make himself behave properly even in the most difficult situations.

He should not agree with his student at all costs. If he sees that his fencer has lost control over his nerves, the coach should relax him and he should only bring up the event and judge it during a training afterwards.

Nonetheless, he should be a suggestive personality, full of vitality, his presence should radiate power and security, and his words should produce excitement. With a fine spirit and a happy mood he can help both himself and his students, allowing the fencing hall to have a good atmosphere.

The major part of the fencing master's physical work takes place during training sessions. The physical work during competitions is nearly zero even if he decides to warm up the fencer with a lesson. The psychological strain of a competion, however, remains high, since only a few people can separate themselves from their student's work. Many coaches fight alongside their students in their minds, which plays on the coach's nervous system, especially during critical bouts.

There are two known ways of becoming a coach. One of them starts with institutional master training, while others (with a longer or shorter amateur past) become coaches through self-development and professional courses. The path to becoming a coach for competitors is always a little more difficult, because their work is not strengthened with the kind of understanding that results from an amateur, recreational past. This is difficult to make up for on the go.

A number of factors influence the evolution of the fencing master's image. These are inextricably intertwined to create the circumstances for someone to be turned into a master. One must find his own way, become polished, and settle down; each step takes a long time and everyone has to go through them.

During their beginner periods, coaches, for a shorter or longer period of time, copy the methods they were once accustomed to. This is not a mistake if they feel that this gives them security to take the first steps. It can be disadvantageous; however, if it impedes that coach's emerging individuality, ties their hands and their imaginations, and relegates their own ideas to the background.

Usually coaches work with one weapon. It is rare for someone to teach even two weapons. The numbers of those who give lessons with both hands, with almost the same quality is even smaller.

Key points about warm-up, training, supervising training sessions, and competitions.

Warm-ups can take place individually or in a group, employing running, running exercises, gymnastics (the general warm-up exercises for almost all sports), special exercises, footwork, target exercises, a lesson given by the coach before or during competitions (this can be substituted with partners assisting each other for the simplest attacking-defending actions), and with actual fencing. In the end, this last option sorts out and coordinates the necessary tools for a successful start.

The basic exercises are the number one item for the beginners' warm-up. The repertoire for advanced fencers and competitors is narrower; their warm-up relies on fencing-specific exercises, except during the period before a new season, when the preparatory physical conditioning takes place.

The range of exercises for the warm-up of the muscles and joints of the lower limbs is wider. The exercises for the upper limbs, the hands, fingers, the arms, rely mainly on the technical elements that take place in front of the target.

The borderline between general and special warm-up is stronger for beginners, but disappears in time. The spectacular elements gradually disappear, giving room for solutions with specific aims, which are unique to each person and prepare the fencer mentally and physically for the beginning of the bout. Since this cannot be achieved by exercises alone, a fencer may fence a bout as a complete warm-up or turn to a bout as a supplemental warm-up before competitions. The last touches during these bouts serve as control for the imagined or real forms.

Beginners usually warm up under the coach's leadership. For more advanced fencers and competitors, this becomes impossible because of their varying time of arrival at the fencing room. After a certain point, warm-up becomes a personal matter regarding its length, intensity, and method. Besides the person's belief and routine, it also depends on the fencer's changing and diversified daily disposition. That is the reason why the coach does not have a say in a steady competitor's warm-up.

Fencers who need more active warm-up are those:

- Who do not warm-up easily
- Who seem indifferent and cannot wind up themselves for a bout
- Who have too much stage fright
- Who have stiffer muscles
- Who tend to become tense between rounds and bouts
- Who quickly lose the effect of the warm-up

Taking into consideration that throughout a competition one has to warm up a number of times, as well as the fact that to some extent, part of the warm-up can be taken in the first bouts (depending on the fencer's talent and the level of the competition), the fencer should always choose the most advantageous and economical warm-up, especially in the case of competitions that take several days.

Factors influencing warm-up include:

- The place of the competition, is it familiar or unfamiliar
- The temperature of the hall
- The tendency of the fencer to be injured
- The importance of the competition to the fencer
- The quality of the competition
- The current shape of the fencer, the level of his toughness, his condition
- The fencer's attitude towards warm-up, need

for it, his understanding of it, the place of the warm-up in the fencer's routine
- The fencer's nervous make-up, his ability to compensate for the excitement of the competition

A coach with multiple fencers in a competition has only a limited opportunity to give lessons. Furthermore, since the bouts generally start later than scheduled, the effect of the lessons may approach zero. In any case, when warming a fencer up with a lesson, the coach should choose actions that are often used by the student. He should try to boost the student's self-confidence and avoid direct and excessive correction.

Competitors relax between rounds and bouts, and they only do a few moves to get ready prior to being called onto the strip.

There are two effects of warm-up: it mobilizes the energies for greater performance, and on the other hand, it reduces and sometimes totally stops the negative factors.

Soccer may have goalie, field, and physical conditioning coaches. In fencing, however, the tasks of technical and tactical training, physical condition training, psychological preparation, and the need to achieve the desired form in the required time – all of these are all in the hands of one person. Among students with different age groups, background knowledge, and skill levels, only the time periods, the proportions, and the main points differ to a smaller or larger extent.

The nature of the sport gradually points out the importance of the competitor's individual and customized preparation. (The coach can begin to gather this information towards the end of group training.) The methods applied cannot be the same for everyone, both for the material and the extent of the load. For some, the development of speed brings the desired results. Others reach this with loose lessons, where the cadence keeps changing. The daily disposition of the students can also influence this question, besides their relation to the sport, their temperament, or their physical abilities. A coach with a system sees the needed signs for disposition at the beginning of the lesson.

For example, if the student is mentally tired, we should burden their physique and the opposite way around. We should not overburden those in a weaker state (unless this is our intention). If necessary, we should help the student by creating the necessary conditions for the successful completion of an action. But we should gradually decrease this help, and we should only return to helping the student when serious mistakes occur.

On a student's "up" day, we should steer the training accordingly. On such days, we should set obstacles to be overcome for a competitor who is able to think and act in alternatives and is able both to keep his attention at a high level and at the same time to divide it. Monotonous, refrain-like repetitions should be avoided. The material should be diverse (diversity is not only attractive and entertaining exercise, it also requires more attention) and the pace should be pulsating. Loose parts, close to resting should alternate with parts with more workload – similarly to how it happens in bouts and at competitions.

Numerous factors have to be taken into consideration during training sessions. There are more variables than constants among these factors, more difficult to detect than easy to see, more hidden and potential circumstances than ones that appear early and give signs. Often a coach has to search for ways to bring about change, because usually the student does not know the sources of the problem. A change of mood or a deteriorating frame of mind that are there from the beginning of the lesson can have bigger effects than many other factors. The ability of the coach to use his instincts in such occasions elevates the coach's work to a type of art.

Training the physique

To train the *physique*, one has to pick such sports, or elements of sports, which do not contradict the nature of fencing too much, but still require the mobilization of various abilities. Out of the sports at our disposal, the ones that have to be forgotten are those that cannot be adapted at all, like triple jump, shot-put, javelin throw, or discus throwing; those that are fixed forms, repeat the same movement for a long time, and have cyclic movements, like paddling, long distance running, swimming, or cycling; and the sports that the student does only reluctantly. And finally those, that can lead to fencers' injuries, such as volleyball, wrestling, boxing, or weightlifting. At the same time, we can turn to soccer (in the form of five-man or indoor soccer), often preferred by fencers, basketball or one touch games for pairs, as long as there is a possibility for them. Before a season, tennis is also a good choice, but once the season begins, only games resembling or built on fencing are justified.

Developing technique

Because of the high level of mobility witnessed in the sport nowadays, many observers, question the importance of the *development of technique*. Nevertheless, since all of the laws that are built on technique are still in effect, technique must be continued being taught even in the future.

One of the difficulties of learning technique is that it requires more attention from the beginning (fencing technique is more like playing the organ than playing the piano), but at the same time it is provided with less excitement when it comes to the body, the movements, and the entertainment value. This is especially hard on children. For children, technique must be taught with the use of pauses, in short series, with exercises leading up to it, and embedded into fencing oriented games. The coach must understand the rule of gradation, know the age-related skills of the students, and possess a strong pedagogical sense.

We should be careful with splitting exercises into parts, or we will lose the important aspect of their coordination and combination into one whole, which is the key to success. If someone repeatedly practices something broken into short parts, that slight pause between parts can happen when actually executing the learned action. This can be enough to prevent the action from fitting into a tempo, or to become a problem in executing an advance without being noticed.

We should not think of the military command as the only trigger for a start of an exercise or movement. This can only help the student to be explosive, and will not guarantee good technique, especially if there is no correction. If someone practices something based on a command for a long time, he becomes comfortable; he loses independence, so much so, that even as a competitor, he will expect the command from his coach, which will be much less useful than before.

Developing tactics

We should combine the training of tactics and technique as much as possible. The explanation of the execution of the action, as a matter of fact, is already a preliminary sign of tactics. In time, this will have to be solved with concrete actions. The difficult part in this is when the student has the initiating role.

We should follow Aristotle's golden mean during the training of tactics. As the number of variables increase, the speed of the execution decreases in direct ratio. We should only work with two variables, or at most three. This can be solved by a person with medium talent, even if the forcefulness and determination are not always as much as they should be.

Technique alone cannot defeat a wily tactician. In the long run, a fencer needs a sense of tactics and the abilities connected to this, which decide the fate of bouts. None of these can be produced and fed into students artificially; only the consistency of the fencer's already existing skills can be developed. (No private can become a commanding general if all he can do is to handle his weapon correctly and according to the rules.)

Based on the above, the ability to learn tactics should be

placed at the center of the search for talent. Since tactics cannot be (and never will be) the first step of training, we have to wait for the proper time.

The enviable abilities of a fencer with good tactics are his calmness, courage to take risks, venturing, thinking in terms of alternatives. Only talented people are capable of deceiving their opponents, making them believe things that the fencer has no intentions of doing. They are the ones who can place themselves in the minds of their opponents, see their cards ahead of time, and beat them from the very outset. They are the people who are able to pull off outrageous ideas, stand on the edge in a losing situation, think and act in fortune-changing ways, and what is more, even to use blind luck for their benefit.

This peculiar faith must be taught during training – this integral self-confidence that allows them never to lose faith in victory and leads to the ability to shut out distractions like the psychological influences of previous losses to the same opponent or the referee's errors, making it possible for them to fight until the very end. Therefore it is an error to believe that psychological preparation is a separate entity, an independent area, one that can be broken away from fencing training, and could be solved by an outsider.

Timing of peak form

Timing of peak form is one of fencing's sore spots. One of the most difficult tasks is coming into peak shape, reaching the upper border of possibility in regard to all of the factors that contribute to fencing performance. Even competitors who can instinctively sense their shape, condition, cannot often give a sure opinion on this question. It is an especially ungrateful task for coaches to issue solid statements regarding the expected results to each of their students.

Furthermore, in fencing, shape and the result rarely overlap each other perfectly. A person thought to be in good shape before a competition can perform inadequately. Conversely, a weakly prepared fencer can achieve results that contradict his shape.

The representatives of sports that can be measured are in an easier situation. Their performance during training is more or less what comes back during competitions. The difference can be bigger in fencing.

Since the measurable components of fencing (leg strength, reaction time, etc.) are only a small slice of fencing shape, fencers and coaches must rely on individual experimentation. There are some do light moves the day before a competition, while others stay away from fencing for 1-2 days before a competition to increase their hunger for the blade.

Because of the high degree of concentration that goes hand in hand with competition, fencers need a longer period to relax after a season. This is why a recovery interval – totally free of professional work, mutual work, teammates, and the use of the fencing hall – has to be inserted between two seasons (this can even be 4-5 weeks; based on the person, coach, competitor). This can even mean the entire avoidance of sport exercise for 2-3 weeks. The physical loss that a fencer faces during this period is amply compensated by the recharging of the nervous system.

There are also various possibilities for easing the tension during a season. We can talk of a proportional decrease in training work, duration, amount, and intensity, changing the methods of exercising, program changes, allowing games at the end of training, decreasing the number of competitions, and – going to extremes – even 1-2 days' absence from training.

Athletes dedicated to fencing have to expect a long preparatory period. This is natural in light of the nature of the sport. Because of the fast pace of life, the feeling for faster appearance, participation, and progress, it will become increasingly necessary for coaches to search for practical solutions that shorten the duration for someone to become a fencer, even though there is no method guaranteed to quickly place someone among the elite fencers.

III. Methods of Conveying Information

Fencing knowledge can be introduced to the student during training through advance explanation and through demonstration.

The plastic, tangible *explanation* should be authentic and convincing. It should evoke interest, grab the students' attention, and turn on their fantasy. It should build on the special characteristics of their ages and their backgrounds. We should not resort to expounding various rules before those who are unfamiliar with them. A different method must be used to talk to them about angular velocity, the advantages of forward parries, differences in leverage, the notion of the shortest distance between two points, or the law of action and reaction. We should attempt to approach these abstract concepts from the direction of practice.

From time to time we should word things from a different aspect, containing practical similes. The most important exercises should be emphasized and highlighted through tone of voice and the use of gestures.

We should articulate and speak with a varying volume. Nothing is more disappointing and soul-destroying than a dull tone. We should phrase things briefly, concisely, straight to the point, and clearly differentiated. We should postpone longer explanations until we are teaching tactics; first, because by that time, the students will be over their initial difficulties and they will know the vocabulary, and second, becausetactics immediately require a wider theoretical range.

We can convey information in verious ways: descriptive, analytical, explanatory, commanding, correcting, detailed, or summary. Material that was initially discussed in general terms must gradually expand to contain all of the nuances.

The best solution for illustrating the complicated space, time and dynamic components of the sport is the *live demonstration*. Other visual tools like movies or photographs cannot replace this during the beginning of the teaching. Pictures and magazine photos of fencing scenes are often useless for teaching since they mainly or solely mirror acrobatic actions and extreme postures of fencers in an emergency, or because the pictures try to capture marginal events (e.g., the arguments between competitors and the jury).

Silent movies rob the viewer of the sound effects connected to the various actions. Modern educational movies with music tracks leave the viewer guessing regarding the rhythm of the fencing movements. We can use videos later, to analyze tactics, when the competitors no longer become surprised when seeing scenes that convey unique stylistic elements.

The ideal – that all the students will see everything properly – cannot be followed in reality. During the first demonstration, we should gather the students around us so they can observe the required actions from multiple sides.

For the better use of time, it is useful to do the repeated demonstrations during practice in front of a straight line of students. The distance from the students should be based on available space and the length of the line of students.

Actions with weapons can be slowed down as desired; they can even be stopped at any point. Some phases can be achieved, for illustration purposes, only with the help of the wall bars, a partner, or holding the student's hand, if we wish to observe them adequately.

We only depict the classical movements ("gymnastics") when warming up with a group. This method cannot be applied for exercises that have aims or are used to lead up to something else.

Since the coach cannot conveniently switch hands when using a pistol grip, we talk about mirror-like demonstration when the master and the student are same-handed (right-

right or left-left). Here, the master uses his unarmed hand to repeat some of the actions, using the outstretched index finger to simulate the weapon and its point. If the coach and fencer use the same hand, the fencer must adapt what he sees to his own side. After a short while this will not cause problems for any student. Of course, if the coach and student are opposite-handed, the demonstration is mirror-like from the beginning.

We can talk about realistic, representative, comparative, analytical, copying, and caricaturing demonstrations. A realistic demonstration is one that looks like real fencing. A representative demonstration is outstanding and perfect. The comparative demonstration compares correct and incorrect technique, while the analytical type focuses on one aspect of the movement. The copying demonstration imitates the movements of a student to point out a mistake or portray the perfection of a movement. (In this last type, the students figure out the correct moves by seeing the wrong ones.) One must keep in mind the aim when choosing between these types.

As we demonstrate, we enhance the parts of the whole without changing their relations. If necessary, slow down the action. Use both hands for illustration. Where the opponent's blade is also needed, turn to the help of the student's blade.

In actual practice, we usually combine the processes for conveying information. Although the shortest verbal explanation is longer than the longest practical demonstration, we try to synchronize the two types of methods. (We have to word things briefly on such occasions.) We save time using words and actions in parallel; we give more emphasis and tone to what we say, while at the same time we can serve the interests of both those whose learning style tends to be auditory and those who are more visual.

Forms of exercises. Guiding principles of collective work. The notion, types, and content requirements of the lesson. Criteria for the coach's footwork and the activities with weapons.

Teaching and training when the coach is working with several students at the same time is what we call group work. The aim is to build the foundation, to teach the alphabet (though complex actions can also be taught in groups).

The most effective work takes place with up to 10-15 people. As the head count grows larger, the work becomes more tiresome and more impersonal, and the coach's voice will suffer from the unavoidable background noise.

In the simplest version of group work, fencers usually work alone, standing in line next to each other. If the size of the group is too big or the space is too small, we can add another line behind the first one, with the students in the second row shifted, so no one is directly in front of anyone else. Lefties should be situated at the end of the line – to their left (the coach's right). The coach should demonstrate the exercises standing in front of the lefties. He should stand there also when he is acting as the opponent while practicing exercises connected to keeping the distance.

This is how we teach the basic position, the on guard, the salute (only the simple version of this nowadays), the self-contained exercises and those that lead up to another movement. (A self-contained exercise teaches a movement by creating the required physical conditions for that movement, while an "exercise leading up to another movement" focuses on one part of a technical element, so the student notes it correctly, thus succeeding in the technical work he is practicing.) Footwork, the invitos (invitation or parry positions), and the straight thrusts – in other words, everything that is the prerequisite of a lesson and the use of a blade – all these are taught in group work.

There are two basic types of practice:

1. Each action cue is provided by the coach. He can give commands with words, instructions, sound signals, or separate or combined movements of the hands or arms. Students have to look out for slight differences between successive signals, and students must finish their actions in sync with the end of the signals or by the time the given command has been said.

   The advantage of this variety: it is easier to monitor, arrange, and control the group, to keep order and make the students behave, to monitor the quality of work, and reach the expected intensity.

1. The coach only tells the students what they have to do. He explains and demonstrates the action and how to perform it. After this, however, everyone works separately. Students pick the load, the proportion of work and rest, and the start and stop times on their own. This program should encompass actions that the students are familiar with.

   The advantages of this variety:
   - The coach is not tied down to one spot. He can to walk among the students, walk behind them. (This is necessary sometimes for correcting some mistakes.)
   - The coach can correct mistakes directly, with the blade and the hands, not only with words.
   - The general correcting comments can be adapted to a given student.
   - Students will learn to work independently, to economize their strength, pay attention to their movements, control them personally, and master their fatigue. Meanwhile the coach can learn about the students' relation to the sport: their diligence, their immediate "talent," their longer-term fencing potential, and the likelihood for a student to stay.

- From time to time, the coach can stand in front of a student, allow the student to hit him, give the blade, or create the necessary conditions for the execution of an attacking or defending action. Such personal assistance and the coach's helping blade motivate a person for concentrated work. At the same time it can give the student a perspective of the future: the individual lesson, for which group work is only a preliminary requirement.

A more advanced form of group work is when students work in pairs. (Working in pairs within a group class is the student's first real encounter with the essence of fencing, the basics of the use of the blade.) One member of the pair does attacking exercises, the other, defending ones. The exercises for both members have to be communicated by the coach. We should have the most talented pair demonstrate the exercise. When necessary, we should hold the fencers' hand or their blades to help with the technical execution. (We can do this under the name of correcting mistakes later, as we walk among the pairs.) If we have a talented student, we can demonstrate the upcoming activities with his assistance and cooperation.

- We can work with constant or changing pairs. If possible, fencers of the same handedness and height should work together. We thus reduce beginner problems with keeping the distance, and we do not have to continuously refer to the differences regarding those with opposite hands.
- We can pair up students with similar or different skills. The former method helps the faster development of the good fencers, the latter helps the weaker students in catching up.

Variations of working in paired groups:

1. This exists in theory, but it is not used too much in practice. This is a type when the coach dictates the steps one after another in the proper order, telling which line what to do, as in the following examples

    I.
    - Coach: "Line A, on guard! Line B, middle distance, on guard, seconde invitation!"
    - Coach: "Line A, extend your arms and hit with a direct thrust with lunge; One! (i.e. 'Go!')"

    II.
    - Coach: "Line A, on guard!" (Or, "Line A, on guard in high line!") Line B, middle distance, sixte invitation!"
    - Coach: "Line B, quarte beat, direct thrust with lunge and hold the lunge position; line A, short retreat and parry quarte. Go!"
        - "One!" Line A ripostes with extended arm,
        - "Two!" Both lines: back to on guard, etc.

2. With advanced fencers, we should only communicate the exercises. The mistakes can be corrected while the coach is walking around the pairs.

Allowing free fencing earlier than it should be leads to many bad habits and leaves much room for improvement. However, we should take into consideration the principle of *quid pro quo* and not refuse to include it within the repertoire when it comes to group work. Towards the end of the season, if not sooner, we should allow our students to try out their strength against each other in this field as well. (A bout is a real test; it gives a purer picture of aptitude for fencing.)

These first combats should be instructed. Give conditions; i.e. "Don't beat the blade, try to hit! (Maximum one beat!) After a parry, riposte immediately! Do not stay in one spot, move your opponent! Vary the size of your steps and the length of the pauses!" etc. The bouts should be split up into segments. We should allow our students to advance towards the real requirements of a bout by giving newer and newer aspects for them.

Practices in which the students follow the coach's personal instructions should be dominant in the beginning. These should be spiced up with paired exercises and solo work. (Youngsters prefer to work in pairs, under the guidance of the coach, than on their own.) Towards the end of the season the proportion should be switched; the dominant paired work and solo exercises should be spiced up with group work.

The efficiency of collective work can be enhanced by:

- Deliberate organization
- Proper use of time
- Teaching independence
- Keeping the spirit of the contest alive by enhancing rivalry
- Offering diverse material
- Avoiding boredom, monotony, soulless training
- Varying the load
- Changing the methods of exercising
- Satisfying the desire for games at the end of trainings

The individual lesson

The individual lesson is a specific training/teaching method for giving a tutorial and teaching the use of the blade, where the fencing master must play the role of the coach, the partner, or the opponent. He must give a program, create the conditions, correct the mistakes, dictate and adapt, in order to polish skills, technique, tactics, enhance physical condition, and develop talent.

Personal cooperation of this kind is an activity that requires lots of physical work. From this perspective, being a fencing master runs rings around all of the other coaching activities.

Fencers receive lessons according to the order of arrival or of thier importance. A lesson starts with the student saluting the coach in the basic position. The coach returns it (these are the formal prerequisites of a lesson), then orders the student to stand on guard (the coach corrects the position). Then the actual lesson begins.

At the end of the lesson, after the mutual salute, the coach shakes hands with the student, who thanks the master for the work.

The lesson:
- Gives style, form, and character to a fencer's movement
- Requires the fencer to become accustomed to changing conditions and thus creates a type of adapting mechanism
- Develops most of the abilities in actual association with one another
- Gives a boost and reason for the fencer to find his unique way of expressing himself

It provides far-reaching opportunity for:
- Customized work
- Individual treatment
- Becoming familiar with the student from all aspects
- Threshing out the smallest details of technique and tactics
- Varied use of the methods

The lesson is determined by the coach's:
- Technical preparedness
- Feel for tactics
- Creative imagination
- Ability to adapt
- Strength

The atmosphere of the lesson is influenced by the coach's personal characteristics. Success depends on how well the coach and the student are used to each other, understanding the signs and signals and the capability to respond to them.

The lesson should be customized, taking into consideration the student's:

- Age
- Background knowledge
- Fencing experience

The lesson should be appropriate to the length of the season and the placement and dates of the important competitions.

Although the profile of the lessons is composite, we can talk of ones that are:

- Analytical or comprehensive
- Educating or focused
- Technical or tactical
- Designed to develop specific skills and abilities
- In addition, physical conditioning, to varying degrees, is a task included in most lessons

The main points of the lesson determine its style. On an advanced level, the profile can change during a lesson. From the basic, classical technical lesson, a number of transitions lead to the silent lesson, which is the most difficult lesson type, where both the coach and the student have to perform their best.

Even the simplest lesson is built on assumptions and, at a basic level, models actual fencing situations. The standard conditions lead to stability; the variables help make the skills flexible. You can give all of the technical and most of the tactical elements in a lesson.

Prerequisites for the *technical lesson* include basic footwork, at least advance, retreat, lunge, and the backward recovery to guard from it, and the direct thrust that was practiced on a target beforehand. Its aim is to give a grasp of technique through the learning of actions occurring in foil fencing.

We should vary the attacking and the defending actions according to the characteristics of the weapon. Change the distance and the intensity as well. Through breaks (we can talk about relaxing breaks, ones intended to raise the attention, and ones used for correcting the mistakes) we should give the lesson a pulsating, periodic character.

Figure 4

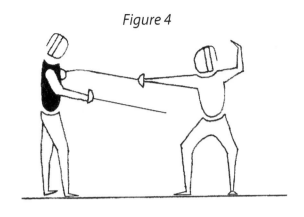

Figure 5

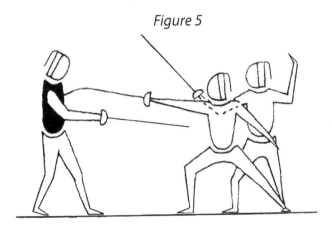

We can perfect the technique of the hand and the arm from close distance (Fig. 4); from the middle and long distances, we can perfect the coordination of the hand and the feet (Fig. 5). Lunges and fleches done from one spot (immobility) teach the fencer how to launch them forcefully. A lesson with motion accommodates a student to keeping the distance, the use of methods to increase the distance, and how to develop and execute actions while in motion.

Practicing in one's own tempo helps creating the best prerequisites for the execution, beginning from a sign helps in using the given possibilities quickly.

Defense without retreat increases parrying skills. Counterattacks heighten the reflexes and shorten reaction time.

The aim of the *tactical lesson*: prepare for combat with an opponent. Its prerequisite is technique that is close to errorless. The coach's job is creating the situation and correcting the tactical mistakes. (In such lessons, we only correct technical mistakes if those influence the tactical execution.)

In this type of lesson, the student practices the possibilities dictated by a given situation. Since the tactical situation always offers more possibilities than are worth working with (speed is proportionally decreased by the number of alternatives), the number of variables must be set up according to the student's abilities. The fencer's habits influence the proportion of offensive or defensive intentions; the strong characteristics of a fencer influence his style. It is the coach's job to create an acceptable balance between the extremes.

The things learned during lessons cannot be used in reality in the same exact way. Every opponent is different and the situations are only similar to each other, not identical. It is enough for one component to change for a learned rule to lose its effectiveness. Matters can take a 180-degree turn.

The probability of success cannot be calculated in advance, cannot be taken for granted as a 100% certainty. There are elements of uncertainty even in the greatest plans. The opponent can figure out anything, he can counteract everything. Tacticians who use more phrases can tolerate this creatively. For people with such gifts, the given tactical lessons are at most a finger exercise, like that for a musician.

Strong boundaries cannot be drawn in reality between the *lesson's introductory part, its main part, and the concluding part*. In the work of experienced coaches, the contours are hazy; the parts melt into each other without any breaks. We find separation only in the works of beginner coaches.

The job of the introduction is to create rapport, tuning in psychologically, warming up the nerve tracks (the coach "tunes" himself to the new student, his abilities, wavelengths, while the student "tunes into" the exercising methods with their specific requirements), and for the coach to discover what the fencer is capable of on that specific day when it comes to technique, tactics, and condition. (These also influence the material and the length of the lesson.) The lesson must usually be set up quickly due to the large number of students.

The main part, 90-95% of the lesson, is the core, which can be used for:

- Expanding the repertoire, learning new variants
- Smoothing the technique
- Repeating, analyzing, maintaining the skills learned so far
- Complex skill development
- Conditioning
- Adapting; practicing alternatives

The concluding part is a closing harmony, a symbolic closure. We usually finish the common work of the coach and the student with 2-3 simple actions, generally with direct thrusts.

The lesson, like a bout, consists of the conversation, the dialogue of two fencers. The difference is that this is a controlled conversation, led by the coach with his student following his thoughts and ideas. The coach dictates, creates situations, asks "questions," corrects the "conditions," narrows or expands the message according to necessity.

Economy and reality are the basic criteria for creating the necessary conditions for the execution of an action. Striving for this, the coach:

- Should turn his upper body in on guard position, as much as the weapon type requires. A larger surface than average does help some thrusts to hit easier, but at the same time it changes the angle where the attacking blade and the target area should usually meet at the moment of the thrusts.
- If the coach stands in one place, his on guard position should be light, natural, and narrow. The feet should be almost parallel to each other; they should stand at an acute angle. His knees

should be loose; his weight should be placed on the front leg. The elbow of his weapon arm should be pulled closer to his hip than a fencer holds it. His weaponless hand and arm should be prepared for work, intervention, help, mistake correction, and demonstration.

- If he wishes to play with the distance, he should sit into the on guard according to the momentum of the movement. The stance becomes wider and the angle made by the feet opens more. This angle still should not reach 90 degrees even with the fastest movement.
- The rhythm of the coach's movements should be so good that it is worth copying.
- The use of the weapon should comply with the formal requirements. The proper grip, and the way it is held and used should be good enough for every student to copy.
- The coach should assist the student by using the converse of dictated actions:
  - To teach the parry, he should attack.
  - To teach the attack, he should open a line.
  - To teach second intention, he should counterattack.
  - To teach counterattack, he should
    - Raise or withdraw his arm
    - Start with the feet, or
    - Begin actions with obvious and large movements.
  - To teach feint attacks, he should play the role of a defender who relies on parries.
  - To teach attack in foot tempo, he should use a long, obvious step forward.
  - To teach the remise, he should pause in the parry position (hold the parry) or avoid the attacks by taking long steps backward.

- To teach bind thrusts and flanconades he should give a rigid blade, like a rail. As the student's blade approaches, he should allow the wrist to break and move away from the thrusting blade in the proper moment.

- In short, the coach should imitate the usual antecedents, reactions, and consequences.

- The coach should imitate a sincere attempt to hit, even though the point must stop a centimeter in front of the target surface. (This is of course indispensable if the student is working without his jacket.)

- The coach's point when attacking should aim within the valid target area (except during the initial movement of the coupé) and it should point towards the desired spot, surface, sector.

- The cues for the student have to be realistic even during exercises that require choices (alternative exercises). Pointing out the differences between the alternatives should not be over-exaggerated. It is better to wait for the students to become mature for this type of practice.

- For beginners, ideal circumstances should be created. The coach should facilitate the student's actions by the use of his blade. However, he should not exaggerate the key elements. For example, the coach should raise his blade to an angle that facilitates the student's attack on the blade, but narrow the angle as the student progresses.

- Competitors, on the other hand, should sometimes be placed in rather uncomfortable situations, e.g., to continue the previous example, the coach should hold the blade flat when asking for an attack on the blade from an advanced student.

- Play into the hands of beginners. Take part in the technical execution and its success indirectly by creating advantageous conditions so that the student can execute the actions correctly.
- Act more like an opponent than a coach when working with competitors. (At the top of the lesson hierarchy is the silent lesson, so to say a symbolic bout.)
- For beginners, use footwork with the same characteristics as the student's footwork. Answer classical steps with classical steps and cross-steps with cross-steps.
- For competitors, on the other hand, the coach can use cross-steps to increase the speed of the student's retreat with classical steps.
- An attack should be signaled with a quarter or half-sized lunge. If age, condition, or physical state does not allow this, the lunge may be replaced with an extra step forward.
- The beginning student should become accustomed to launching his action according to a live signal, instead of launching the actions either in his own tempo or on the coach's verbal command. However, verbal cues may be associated with other fencing signals, but only for a short time. Later only the signals themselves will be enough to produce the required reflexes.
- On an advanced level, footwork and giving the blade become launching signals instead of part of the background.
- Avoid sudden, unexpected, push-like cues. Wait until attention is at its highest level before beginning the action (wait for this for a longer time if necessary). If needed, be prepared to give a hint for the beginning of the action. This helps beginner students.

- The invitations and their variations should finish with the hit, thus illustrating a proper hit in a tempo.
- Insert pauses between giving blades. The pause can be a moment used to relax the fencer, increase his attention level, give emphasis to something, allow preparation, signal a change in action, separate the elements of a series, demonstrate the phase-like characteristic of the sport and its varying levels of tension.
- Use the unarmed hand and arm for demonstration and mistake correction, illustrating the direction of the fencer's movements, increasing attention, and giving assistance.
- The signaling system should be clear and obvious. Do not change the meaning of the cues: it should be consistent, so that the coach can expect his students to act without hesitation.
- Give time for the students to become used to the launching signals, the signals aimed to correct mistakes, and the signals used to comment on something.
- Learn how to give an expressive, differentiated blade while working in a narrow amplitude.
- Strive for extensive economy of movement and energy; otherwise it is impossible to give 6-8 lessons a day.
- Avoid theatricality. Get rid of annoying movements, the coaching blunders that might result in incorrect reactions on the student's part.
- The most common bad habit is the strong upbeat on the student's blade after the hit. This is a useless waste of energy. Because every action has a reaction, the students usually stiffens, counters, opposes these late and drastic "parries," which lead to technical mistakes in execution. If the aim of this movement is to correct

the touch's end position, to adjust the student's hand, the movement used should be a pushing, pressing motion. Also, a slight beat on the student's blade, after the touch, can replace the "On guard!" command. The coach can send the blade or the student back into the starting position this way.

- The strong "coach's beat" should only be part of the repertoire if intended to imitate a late parry, as a tool for speeding up the attacking blade. This requires that the attacking and defending blades must meet at the proper time, place, and with the proper strength.
- When changing actions within the lesson, and when ending the lesson, the practice should be ended with successful actions by the student.

Not all coaches are successful in both group training and individual lessons. Some like both types equally and are able to do them with almost the same quality. Some can be good in only one of the methods. However, since in practice most coaches have to raise the rising generation on their own (relatively few are assisted by fellow coaches), a fencing master should be efficient in both forms of teaching.

One cannot write down the material of a lesson ahead of time. Everyone improvises; the actual program is set up both according to what has gone before and what the student brings to the lesson today.

Since a lesson is a daily task, too many students cannot work with one coach. The class size should be set up so that, besides the lessons themselves, there is time left for supervising exercises (footwork, target practice, work in front of the mirror, paired exercises, set bouts, and free fencing).

Learning the methodology of teaching can be best achieved by working with beginners, while the craft of giving the blade can be best learned by giving lessons to technically developed competitive fencers.

The path of forming technique into skill. Tools and their use.

Technique must be taught partly in a linear way and partly along a rising spiral. Repetitions that come back like the chorus of a song – interspersed newer and newer elements which act as its verses – are required for perfecting the details and the ability to adapt to changing conditions. The actions have to be built up loosely, not too strictly or rigorously at first. The details have to be perfected later on.

The order of the actions that are to be taught must be arranged by the principle of going from easy to difficult. Since there is no absolute order for this, the coach must be guided partially by the order laid out in textbooks and partially by common sense.

Actions first taught formally should only gradually be filled out with dynamics. Technical proficiency should be the goal at the outset, when the emphasis should be placed on light, loose movements. Until proficiency is attained, speed and explosiveness should not be forced, and the actions must not be changed or developed.

There are few plausible, evident, and natural elements in fencing (the on guard position is constructed already), so as long as it is necessary, the coach can try to help the students with the use of self-contained exercises, exercises leading up to another movement, and exercises that force them to do something in a given way, or with the use of various tools, such as the wall bars. The more talented fencers and the ones with better technical skills need less of such exercises or none at all, but less coordinated students, beginners, and children are more likely to need to rely on them.

Difficult movements should be simplified, and approached in a natural way if possible.

Beginning students should be simply placed into the unfamiliar stances and positions (i.e. basic or on guard positions). (Ballet dancers do the same thing.) None of the fencing nations use elaborate academic sequences to achieve these positions any more.

Movements that are easy to imitate, i.e. step forward and backward, should be taught as a whole, just as parents do not teach their children to walk in half-steps.

The more difficult parts of actions should be practiced by the students ahead of time, i.e. the recovery from the lunge, in the form of asymmetrical gymnastic exercises – the order of the two hands and the two arms and their movements following one another at different times.

In order to emphasize the lifting of the toe in the step forward, step backward, and step forward – lunge, the student should place the point of the blade between the big toe and the next one, then press the blade upward (it should slightly bend, the bend itself should point forward and it should not change). The students should do a few movements this way.

Binds should be taught from contact. Beats, after showing them personally, should be taught in the form of counter beats, sometimes even doubled.

We should place tennis balls in the hands of the fencers when teaching the fleche. (They should throw the ball forward and downward, catching it on the bounce with a fleche.)

Before resorting to exercises with weapons, the students should do the motion of the simple, semicircle, and circle parries, while using both of their hands and arms through the use of complex gymnastic exercises. The students should follow the verbal commands and the coach's movements. We should first stick to the rudimentary vocabulary and we should move on to the advanced terminology later on.

Teaching the positions should proceed as follows:
- "Stand sideways, with your knees bent and your feet parallel and slightly separated!"
- "Lift both arms sideways, slightly above horizontal!"
- "Bring your hands together, as if you were praying!" (This will become quarte.)
- "Open both arms sideways, turning your hands out a little!" (This will become sixte.)

- "Turn your hands inside and downwards in a slight arc!" (This is how a seconde will be done from a sixte), and finally
- "Turn and lift both arms to about the height of the middle of your chest; the palm of the weapon arm should be slightly lower than the other!" (This will be the motion of septime.)
- The semicircular and circular parries can be taught the same way.

Through this exercise, everyone witnesses the parries, their positions and movements, and the left and right-handed parries, all at the same time. Both hands and both arms control each other when it comes to both form and amplitude. In addition, with this method, the saber parries can be situated beside the parries of the thrusting weapons with supinated and pronated hand positions.

(Use the semi-circular and circular transfers to help in teaching the semicircle and circle parries with the use of the weapon.)

Turning technical knowledge into skill is greatly helped by the use of the mirror and the target as tools. (The tennis ball, the bars, and even the weapon itself offer fewer opportunities,) Feedback from mirror and target also facilitates the formation of the sense of our body in motion. Their use depends on how well equipped the fencing hall is, the number of coaches and the number of students, and on the individual's perception and confidence. With their aid, one can work without the coach's presence and direct commands.

The mirror has a controlling role mainly in developing footwork, while the target mainly has a role in developing thrusting technique.

The fencer should be about 2 – 3 meters from the mirror. This is the best way for the student to witness the differences between one's own movements and the correct technique. The use of peripheral vision becomes impossible from a closer range, while details become too small from farther away. The student's gaze should be at the height of the shoulders.

Mistakes connected to holding or moving the weapon and the consequences of an improper fencing line are seen better when facing the mirror (the amplitudes of the invitos and parries can be adjusted to one's body contours). Standing sideways by the mirror allows the person to see mistakes in body position, the position and movement of the non-weapon arm, and the coordination between weapon-work and footwork.

Footwork without a weapon should sometimes be switched to the non-dominant side as well. (This forces a beginner to concentrate more.) Naturally, during such practice, steps and lunges should be shorter, while speed is a secondary consideration.

Several people can work facing the mirror simultaneously if it is large enough. In this case the coach usually directs and helps in the correction of mistakes.

The sense of distance can be refined when practicing on the target, the lengths of short, medium, and long distance for the individual fencer can be established. Different spots can be targeted; standing at an angle to the target surface helps practice confident hitting on an unfavorable surface. The final position of the point signals a miscalculated distance or when the fencer leans into the target at the end of the lunge because of insufficient development of the thigh muscles.

Wall targets should be set up at least 1 meter apart; and if possible, their heights should be different, so even the shortest fencers can find an advantageous "partner" for their height. (This is especially important in case of child fencers.) The difference will not cause problems later. (Round targets with a steep side are better than square targets, and all targets should have a round center patch, preferably of a contrasting color. See illustration, p.6.)

In gyms, the target can be replaced by exercise mats hung on the wall or the bars, by small padded boxes placed on each other at a proper height and leaned against the bars or the wall, or the top of a box standing on end. As a last resort, one can do target exercises on a fencing jacket folded and fastened on the bars.

First, the point should hit while the person is facing the target squarely (Fig. 6). Greater confidence in the point is required for hits starting from a 45-degree angle. In such a case, the target already resembles the narrow profile of an opponent's body.

The starting position can be a line, an on guard in lower or

Figure 6

upper line, or a position with the point placed on the ground. Or the starting position can be one of the invitos (for beginners it should be quarte or sixte). The lateral movements of quarte or sixte can be adjusted to the sides of the target.

Besides the direct thrusts, students can imitate the bind thrusts and the feints formed out of the invitos. (They must outline in the air the circular patch at the center of the target.) The blade should function as a large pencil.

The fencer can practice on a target alone or with a partner. If there are few targets and a large head count; more people can work in a fan-like position. The advantage of the latter is that the distance between the fencers (the higher the head count, the smaller the distance) forces each fencer and his blade to work on a straight line, stabilizing and controlling the position of the torso. When using the fan-like position, occasionally call for a position change; the people standing on the sides should be in the middle and vice versa. Due to the lack of space, the action in such case can be no more than a direct thrust. It is better if the coach dictates this.

When practicing in pairs in front of the targets, one student can assist for beat thrusts. The assistant gives a blade; the partner does a beat and hits the target. The coach can

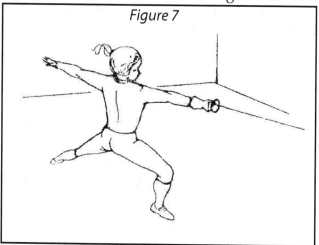

Figure 7

also give competition-like exercises where one person dictates, the other follows; or one initiates, the other adjusts.

Beginners usually start learning the direct thrust by hitting the air (Fig. 7). The disadvantage of this is that since there is no concrete spot that can be targeted, so that the point moves right and left, and the hand and arm do not finish in the proper position. This is why it is better to teach the direct thrusts with the use of a target right from the beginning, without having the students do even one thrust where the point does not hit anything. Coaches can choose from a number of exercises to prepare the students for the direct thrust. Hereafter we will give a taste of such exercises, leaving the variations and combinations up to the coach's discretion. (One should signal if the starting position is not the on guard.)

1. Hit the middle of the target with an extended arm; from step in place, a jump in place, jumps back and forth with some movements, or imitating the cross-steps in place. The torso and the arm should be motionless; the legs should work from the waist down. This exercise should not be measured in minutes, rather in the number of completed sets. After a maximum of 8-10 repetitions, there should be a short pause followed by a new exercise.

2. The same exercise as before, but hit the target with a bent arm. The angle between the upper arm and forearm should not change. Everyone should decide on their own regarding the combinations, how frequently, with what pairs, with how many variables, and how fast a person wants to work, and when and for how long he wants to pause.

3. Hitting the middle of the target with an extended arm, then 2-3 tiny steps forward while the arm steadily bends more and more; then going back to the starting point and re-extending the arm.

4. The same as above, but now it should be done with 2-3 flat jumps both forward and backward while the blade remains touching the target and the arm bends or extends to adjust.

5. The combination of the third and fourth exercises, in which the student advances with steps and retreats with jumps, even if he switches after a whole back and forth step.

6. Hit the middle of the target with an extended arm, step in place with the front leg and slowly move the rear leg into a backward lunge and then back to the starting position.

7. The same exercise as above, but with jumps into lunge and back to on guard.

8. Exercises 6 and 7 combined.

9. Hit the target with extend – lunge. Jump back into on guard and then back into a lunge. Repeat.

10. The starting point is the on guard. The heel of the rear foot should be lifted and turned gradually to reach a backward lunge, and then with the same movement moved back to the starting position.

11. All the above exercises executed from a 45-degree angle from the face of the target.

12. Hit the middle of the target with an extended arm, after slightly bending the arm and lifting the point; repeat the thrust once or twice, hitting the same spot or targeting different spots.

13. The same as above, but launch the first hit (the one before the repeats), from high line or low line.

14. Short distance, on guard in low line or with the point on the floor. Raise it to high line, then direct thrust; or execute the thrust from the floor, trying to hit as quickly as possible.

15. The same exercise done from medium or long distance.

16. From medium or long distance, tap the weapon once or twice on the floor, then lift it into high line and direct thrust, or immediate direct thrust after the beat(s).

17. Starting from considerably out of distance, advance towards the target with steps of different lengths and speeds and hit the target with extension only, extension – lunge, or step forward – extension – lunge (depending on the distance) sometimes changing the place to hit. Change the rhythm with half-steps, retreats, glides, sudden pauses between steps forward or in the movement. By giving lines and changing invitos – like shadowboxing – one can imitate situations from a bout.

18. Two fencers should stand close to each other in front of the target at medium distance. One is the leader, the other the follower. The latter has to follow the leader's movements without any mistakes and with the smallest possible delay. Each mistake scores a point for the leader. After five points, the students should switch

positions and roles. The leader can order
- High or low line
- Simple extension or thrust with lunge
- Remain in lunge for a longer or shorter time
- One or more extra thrusts following a hit

The aim is to be as unexpected as possible and create maximum difficulty for the partner. The leader can give commands from both sides. In the case of same-handed fencers, the follower, standing in front of the leader's chest, has a more difficult job. The follower should use his peripheral vision, whichever side he is working on.

19. Eight to ten fencers should each stand in front of a target, lining up in a row at short or medium distance. The coach should signal the fencer at the right or the left end to do a direct thrust with lunge. As soon as the point hits, the next person launches his lunge. Everyone should stay in the lunge position until the last person finishes. The coach then signals the return to the on guard. The weapon can be launched from different positions, high or low line, invitos, or after one or two beats on the floor.

20. Pairs should work in front of a target. One person should assist in the execution of simple beat thrusts, first on the spot, then by changing the distance, and finally with the use of the tempo taken from the hand. The helper stands next to the partner and moves his blade up and down parallel to the partner's blade. As soon as the moving partner stops or lifted his blade in the proper height, the other person must do the beat thrust.

The bars are a rarely used tool. By holding the bars, however, a coach or a fencer can emphasize, exaggerate, magnify, divide, and practice parts and details of fencing movements that are characteristic components of footwork with respect to rhythm or to formal, dynamic aspects, but which can followed with difficulty or not at all during continuous motion,

(These are especially important for beginner and advanced fencers.)

- *On guard with the fencer's back to the bar and holding on with one hand, or on guard with the upper body fencing the bar and holding on with both hands.* The pointing foot, getting ready to launch a lunge can remain in the air with a pendulum-like movement for a shorter or longer time. It can be paused during a chosen movement, either for demonstration or for practice.

- *From the same positions:* Beginning with one foot already in the air, one can emphasize the placement of the accelerating rear foot on the ground during a step forward or the front foot hitting the ground during a jump forward where the foot is not pointing upwards, but rather the toes are kept close to the ground.

- *On guard parallel to the wall with the upper body turned towards the bars. (Hold on with both hands, arms bent, waist-high.)* From this position a continuous a powerful pulling-pushing, pushing-pulling movement of the arms can speed up the total execution of forward and backward steps (starting practice in this order; the steps should be short for a good rhythm).

- If there are a number of bars next to each other, a student can practice and accelerate the continuous steps forward and lunges (if using only one set of bars, it is unavoidable for the continuity to break because of the necessary steps backward.).

- A series of jumps from a lunge into on guard and from the on guard into a lunge, all while the student is leaning on the bars to lighten the strain on the legs in order to gain speed during the movements. The fencers find themselves using a complete skill- and ability-developing exercise because of the changing of the amplitude, speed, and length of the incorporated pauses.

- Standing with one's back towards the bar, a powerful push from the non-weapon arm at the beginning of the lunge can make a lunge or step forward and lunge explosive.

- Finally, the muscles of the stomach, back, side, and arm can also be developed with the use of the bars. (The possibilities offered by the use of gym equipment are much more than what the sport requires in this respect.)

Besides the mirror, the target, and the bars, a tennis ball and a jump rope can also have a role in training, though less frequently and for shorter periods of time. Their role is more of developing abilities, instead of developing technique.

The development of technique is a process that takes a long time, which can be interspersed with sudden leaps, stagnation, and even setbacks. A coach should be patient. There may be a number of fencers who had difficulty with technique but over time developed into better fencers than some who were called talented from the beginning. That is why one cannot prematurely reach the verdict and the final word that a student is hopeless.

No matter how much the coach tries, technique will be colored with characteristics of individual style. These mirror the individual's morphological capability and body structure, the condition of the muscles and joints (whether they are loose or set), and the student's aptitude (or lack of it) for learning movement. Problems with learning a movement can be ameliorated by exercises that lead up to the final movement. We should give more relaxing exercises as a daily dose for those with muscles and joints that are set and stiff, while we should give more intense exercises for students with a weaker body structure. (We should give these exercises during group work as well.) The results will be far from uniform, but they will bring development for everyone.

We should not bother older competitors (30 years or more) with making up for the missing formal requirements. One should pay more attention to the essential questions.

A fencer only uses part of the existing actions. In general, the core of the training sessions should be the general fighting habit, the style, and the actions connected to one's comprehension. Everything else is a side dish, material that can be chosen, new exercises (the tool for developing skills) or an exercise leading up to another movement.

The theory and practice of correcting mistakes. Individual and combined, positive and negative methods.

Mistakes are a natural by-product of movement learning. Even the most talented fencers cannot really avoid mistakes in their movements, because fencing movements are unusual. Correcting them requires mutual work by coach and student.

Mistakes do not show up only when learning something new; they also appear when repeating automatic movements. One must look out for these as well.

A mistake is the difference between the best theoretical execution and the concrete, practical product. Besides huge, obvious differences, smaller ones can also mar the picture.

The biggest mistakes or those that occur during important actions should be corrected first. Among beginners, the most glaring mistakes are the standard ones.

For example:

- Dragging the rear foot along the ground during the step forward
- Starting the lunge with the knee (that is, lifting the front foot vertically instead of propelling it forward)
- Starting the lunge by swinging the leg backward (far worse!)
- Passivity of the rear leg while recovering from lunge

Correcting mistakes in the starting positions is prevention; by starting with corrections immediately, the coach can head off a number of mistakes that would otherwise occur while moving and the tiresome job of correcting those mistakes afterwards. Mistakes witnessed while in motion have to be pointed out during the execution of the given action. The end position, like the starting position, can be corrected at once.

A cause and effect connection must be sought when several mistakes happen together. Eliminating the primary, causative mistake usually leads to the elimination of the resulting errors without having to correct those separately. For example:

- If a fencer leans into a lunge too much, it suffices for the coach to make him press down his back hip for the end position of the lunge to become ideal, with the shoulders, weapon, and floor being almost parallel.
- In a lunge, if the rear knee turns towards the floor and the foot rolls onto its inner side as well, it is enough to turn the knee towards the proper direction. The foot itself will also be corrected thanks to the correct position of the knee.

The coach's work, when monitoring the student and correcting his mistakes, consists of the following steps:

1. Surveying with the eyes, the ears, and the sense of touch. These senses work together in observing and commenting on the facts, individually or in combination, depending on the distance and the action.
   - We should use our peripheral vision, which allows us to see the whole motion, and is highly sensitive to fast movements on the edges of the field of vision, to follow the rapidly moving body, limbs, and weapon, and to check the coordination between the legs and the hand. We should use our central vision for observing starting positions, static situations, and the varieties of actions.
   - Hearing is a tool for monitoring actions that produce sounds.
   - The sense of touch processes the impressions

that occur when the blades meet (beats, binds, parries).

2. Assessing the mistake (mistakes) results from the comparison of ideal and actual technique and tactics. The mistake can be:
   - Capital or marginal
   - Regarding form or content
   - Sporadic or constant
   - Technical or tactical in nature
3. Setting up the order for correction according to the size or importance of the mistake.
4. Choosing methods of correction:
   Correction can happen:
   - Verbally
   - With our bare hands
   - With the help of a weapon in our hands

   We can correct any mistake from anywhere verbally.

   We can only correct technical differences with our hands or with the blade if the distance is appropriate and we are standing in the proper position.

   We can use 2-3 methods at the same time if our first choice does not work. We save time and energy with this and the expected effect will be greater as well.
5. Executing the chosen method. If we do not achieve our goals, try other methods.

Give positive corrections and remedies, rather than diagnoses. Verbal mistake correction is positive when the coach gives commands in imperative mood, stating what the student has to do to avoid repeating a given mistake again. We should not state the diagnosis ("Your point is drooping; you start with your knee; your lunge is too high; you parry too close to the body," etc.); we should give remedies: "Keep the point up! Parry in front! Start by extending your arm and your blade! Make a smaller parry! Feint longer! Disengage later! Beat stronger!" etc. Since we register what we see and hear instinctively, one should strive to acquire the habit of positive mistake correction – which is undoubtedly more effective – as early as possible.

One must correct the mistakes of beginners and advanced fencers almost continuously. A coach has to talk louder in a noisy fencing hall. (The mask stops a lot of the coach's voice.) Articulate speech is an important requirement.

When leading group work, our verbal corrections should be addressed to the group; they should be impersonal and plural, e.g., "Sit deeper, class! Stand up, people! Shorter steps! Lower your shoulders! Extend your arms from the elbow!" etc.

A co ach and a student who are already used to each other learn to understand one another from simple words (Head! Shoulder! Knee! Elbow! etc.). Beginners, however, often need full sentences so that they know what they have to do.

Besides (or instead of) verbal correction, we can also correct with one or both hands, with the unarmed hand and the blade together, and with the blade alone.

We can correct mistakes with the hand or the blade during group work, if we walk among the students. In such cases we can eliminate two mistakes at the same time (two students making the same mistake or two different mistakes) one mistake manually, the other one with the help of the blade. If the work of the group is led by two coaches, one of the coach's sole job is mistake correction.

Usually we use both hands for correcting mistakes made by the weapon hand and arm, as well as in the execution of binds and parries. We use one hand to fix or immobilize the parts that had no mistakes, while we use the other hand to assist in the student's execution, steering the blade on the desired path, influencing the starting mode, the extension, and the limitation of the amplitude of blade movement as well. This method can be used when we demonstrate the movements for the first time and not only for correcting mistakes. If we have a weapon, we have to hold it so it does not impede our work. When it is time to correct something without the use of the weapon, it is best if we hold it with two-three fingers at the end of the grip, with the grip pressed to the palm and the point hanging down, or we if place it under the arm or in the crook of the weapon arm with the point facing backward. We must not cause any injuries or physical pain to the students when correcting mistakes with the blade. For example, if we wish to correct the knee leaning inward with this method we do not strike the knee; we rather place the blade on the proper part of the knee and press it to the required position. The same method has to be used if we wish to change the plane of the torso, if we wish to get rid of the heightened, tense shoulder from the movement, or if we want the hips to go deeper.

We can correct with hand and the blade without even touching a student. Our signals in such instances are usually additional elements or verbal correction. We can achieve the desired effect without any words, if the students are familiar with the meaning of our movements; that is, if they know what we want to express with them. Rotating one's palms inward and downward, for example, can make the student sit in a deeper on guard; while by rotating the palms outward and upward, we can lift the on guard. With our hands moving away from each other (palms facing outwards) we can adjust the knees in the on guard and move inward-leaning knees outward to their proper position. To give the command for turning the torso more, we should use our hands, chest-high, palms facing each other as if we were holding the torso, and rotate them horizontally. These are basically universal signals that beginner coaches learn quickly. Using them clearly, properly, at the right time, and effectively, however, is a question of continued practice.

Manual correction by the use of the hand(s) and the weapon is the fastest method; the blade functions as an extension of the arm and can reach places which a fencing master could only reach by leaving his place. *However, it cannot be done exclusively.* Sooner or later, verbal instructions will also be required, since one can only use words when we justify, reason, support, emphasize, explain the execution, rate the performance, or approve some movement (partially, these are also the tools of mistake correction).

During a lesson, the coach should only leave his position to correct a mistake if he feels that there are no other possibilities to achieve his aim.

These methods of correcting fencing mistakes cannot be viewed as the only possibilities, and none of them can be regarded as mandatory for a specific error. The coach, who is present in a given situation and sees the whole picture, decides on their deployment. He is the one who knows what, when, and to what extent he wants to bring out a given response from the students. The answer is influenced by the state of the student, whether a beginner or advanced fencer, the number of students in the group or on the floor, the type of exercise, its form, the distance between the coach and the student, the place of the mistake, its size, and its type. The applied methods also mirror the coach's view regarding mistake correction.

General methods for correcting mistakes

- Eliminate the kind of excessive concentration that can become a barrier, produce spastic will, and overwhelm mental-physical effort.
- To loosen tense muscles, relax the conditions for the action. For instance, instead of the coach signaling a tempo, allow the student to begin the action when he feels prepared to execute it.
- With stubborn mistakes that keep on returning, take part in the student's execution of the action. Provide direct help manually and indirect help by giving the blade. Sometimes help with the voice as well.
- Modify the distance, taking into consideration the optimal, the realistic, and the exaggerated possibilities.
- While maintaining the rhythm form, proportionally decrease or increase the speed.

- Emphasize the troublesome parts and have them practiced.
- Take a step back to a lower level in the pattern according to which the actions are built up.
- Use the possibility of exercises that lead the student to do an action, exercises that result in a proper execution of a given action.
- Make the conditions easier or harder. Place a smaller or larger obstacle in the path of the execution. Narrow or widen the path of the blade. Emphasize the incorrect parts.
- Split the actions into pieces; take them apart into elements. (Some coaches use this as their fundamental method from the beginning; others only use it for huge mistakes.)
- Stop in the critical spots, phases, connecting points, for shorter or longer periods of time, and only continue the action once these have been corrected.
- Use the possibility of repeating explanations and repeating demonstrations to serve as an example. Be sure to justify why an action must be executed in a given way.
- In order to create the appropriate mental-physical condition for launching the next action, give more time, a longer breath for preparation, so that the student can digest what he has seen and heard. If necessary, regain the student's attention two or three times before starting again.
- As a counterpart of the correct execution, sometimes show the incorrect, bad one also, even with exaggeration. (Be moderate when caricaturing.) Creating a contrast between the correct and the incorrect can help a lot for people who see and feel their mistakes by seeing the differences.

There are times when the most effective way of demonstrating the consequences of a mistake is to score a touch on him (only do this if the student is wearing a jacket!) This is the most emphatic and startling method of correction.

- If the fencer executes an incorrect attack on the blade, hit him with a stop thrust or a disengagement in tempo thrust.
- If the fencer parries insufficiently, hit him directly.
- If the fencer parries too early, hit him with a feint attack.
- If the fencer starts his attack with the body, or with a retracted arm, or with the feet, hit him with a stop thrust.
- If the fencer holds his parry too long, hit him with a remise.
- Against the fencer who hesitates, hit him with a riposte.
- Finally, if nothing else helps, suspend the practice of movements that lead to failure for shorter-longer periods of time.

First check the starting position, the way the weapon is held, the condition of the muscles, and the level of the student's attention. The action should only be started after this check.

After correcting the major leading mistakes (their disappearance can lead to the elimination of a number of collateral mistakes), we should move on to correcting the minor mistakes.

In practice we mainly correct verbally. There are fewer possibilities for correcting manually and with the blade.

IV. Positions and Their Roles in the Bout

In *basic position*, the fencer turns his torso and head (the weapon hand and arm facing towards the opponent), his feet are positioned in a right angle (heels are touching), and stands relaxed with loosely extended knees (Fig. 8). The two arms can be hanging by the side, or placed on the hips, or held parallel to the ground with the palms facing upwards. If the fencer has a mask and a weapon, then prior to the salute, the weapon must be held horizontally with extended

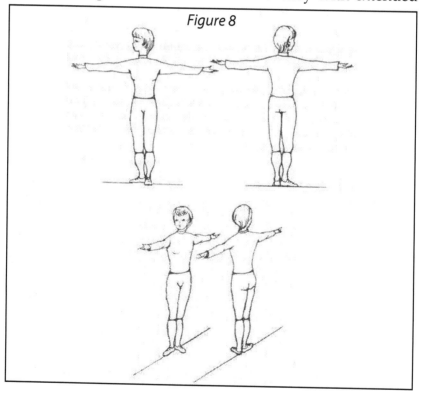

Figure 8

arm, with the mask must held against the body with the non-weapon arm.

In the past, taking up basic position had a strictly defined choreography, which had to be followed by the students under coaches who came from military master training, (institutionalized civilian training barely existed in those times). The basic position was first taught with two cadences and then one, without a weapon and then with a weapon, and finally with mask and weapon in hand. Today, both the sport and its education have stripped their fripperies. Coaches treat the positions, and teach them, based on their importance, and they simply have the students copy them. Since basic position does not influence the bout, it is useless to obsess over its precision.

The *salute*, which begins in the basic position, originally addressed the opponent, the jury, and the audience in a dramatic and elaborate way. A shorter version of this is used nowadays (Fig. 9). In this short salute, the fencer stands in the basic position with a horizontally extended weapon arm, bends his elbow towards himself and extends it once again. It is up to the fencer's own approach if the person leaves the elbow in the original position or if he brings it closer to the body. (In the latter case, the guard rises to the height of the face.) The salute at the end of a bout is followed by a handshake. Today, this handshake is already owed to the referee.

The *on guard* is the symbol of the sport, the beginning of the lesson, practice, and the bout (the *"Fence!"* or *"Allez!"* command is only given once the fencers have taken up this position), and an intermediate stage within these. The competitors launch attacks from this, to this they recover, and from this position they usually defend themselves (Fig. 10). The advantages are the following:

- The length of the weapon arm can be increased by the width of the shoulders.
- One can direct the blade against the opponent with precision.
- The upper body is situated in a position that is

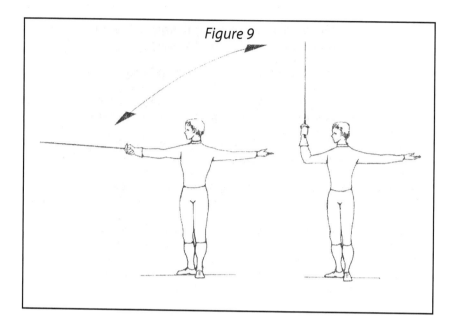

Figure 9

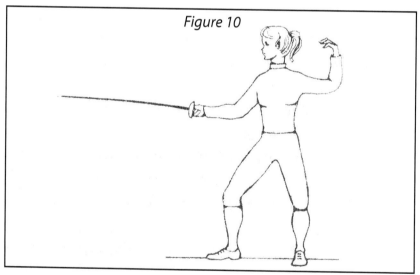

Figure 10

difficult to hit, removing the rearmost parts of the body from the danger of a direct hit.

• The position allows fast movement in both directions.

In order to reach these aims, the fencer places his feet on the ground at a right angle, approximately one and a half times the fencer's foot-length apart. By bending both knees at the same time, he places his torso at the top of the pentagon formed by the legs. His head and his gaze face toward the imaginary opponent (Fig. 11).

A fencer should not only *stand* on his feet: he should *"grip"* the ground, the way an octopus sticks with its tentacles.

The body weight, in repose, is placed on the legs in about a fifty-fifty ratio. This naturally changes during motion. Such a change, however, cannot be conspicuous (unless this is our explicit aim), or detrimental to the fencer's balance or his handling of the blade.

It is pointless to overdo the turning of the torso. It is everyone's own task to find the optimal angle in relation to the fencing line, in which the torso's position not only adheres to the requirements of fencing, but to the fencer's comfort as well. Until the fencer figures this out, however, the coach has a guiding role in this question.

The right angle position of the feet is a classical requirement. Only a few coaches insist on it nowadays. An angle smaller than 90^0 is acceptable. Unacceptable, however, is the backward direction of the rear foot.

The distance between the two feet is an approximate value, which in practice is influenced by the individual's height, the ratio between the torso and the limbs, and the size of the feet.

The exact on guard position – whether it is wider or narrower, higher or deeper – is influenced by the size and proportions of the body, the situation, and the chosen tactics. One can sit deeper in a wide guard and less deep in a narrow guard. The wide one is stable but less mobile and vice versa: the narrow guard is more mobile but less stable. The

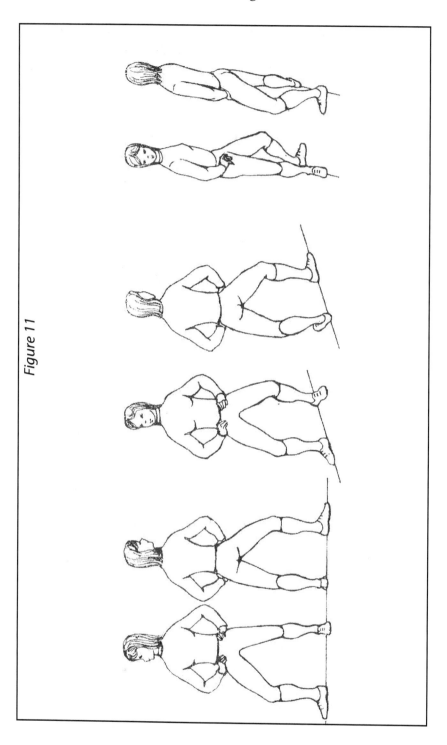

Figure 11

conflicting factors must be balanced as need dictates. In motion, we instinctively ease the strain. We search for a more stable position, a securer base, when preparing to parry. In front of the rear line, for example, we sit deeper than usual, so that in addition to our intention to hold our ground, our on guard position will also help us stay on the strip. (We are harder to move in a wider stance.)

The feet have to be positioned so the heel of the rear foot is covered, hidden when looking at it from ahead. This is when we say that the student is standing on the imaginary line (or rather the imaginary narrow stripe) which is called the *fencing line*. In theory, this is what connects a fencer's two heels, or the four heels of the two fencers facing each other – in cases when the students follow the above-mentioned rules. A coach and his student can check the position of the feet, their placement, and keeping the direction while in motion with the help of this imaginary line. Fencers tend to use this line in bouts also, since this helps to show the smallest profile while facing an opponent and allows the weapon to be directed along the shortest path. At close distance, the requirement for this fencing line ceases to exist, because close combat has its unique requirements for the position of the fencers and for handling the weapon (Fig. 12).

During teaching, we can even draw the fencing line on the floor if necessary. The painted lines in gyms and the sidelines of the strip in fencing halls can make the fencing line visible for students.

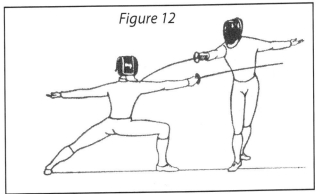

Figure 12

Under ideal conditions and according to classical norms, the knee of the rear leg is situated above the toes, making that like a compressed spring. The knee of the front leg is above the heel and the ankle, with the shin vertical.

It must be noted that we rarely see this classical on guard position these days. Nevertheless, coaches should start by teaching the classical requirements, and not only because the foil fencer's position actually approaches this ideal form. Later, one allows adjustments between the existing best theoretical solution and the individual's physical abilities.

We can take up the on guard from the basic position. In this case the students take a step forward with their front foot to the distance of one and a half, or a maximum of two fencer's foot-lengths, and at the same time, bend their knees and sit into the on guard.

If instruction does not begin with the basic position, the on guard can be taught in the following way:

1. We simply have the students copy our on guard as we demonstrate it. We should not separate the position of the feet and the arms; both should be taught together. (Some coaches, however, have the students place their hands on their hips at first, so it is easier for them to concentrate on the legs only.)

2. The other possibility is to have the students begin by standing in a side straddle, with parallel feet one and a half or two foot-lengths apart. Then we have them bend their knees, keeping their backs straight. Finally the front foot (corresponding to the weapon arm) and the head are turned by 90-degrees. Then the two arms are placed in the on guard position. The advantage of the method is that the body weight, from the first, is evenly divided between the legs (no need to work on this separately), the rear knee's position is also evident, and the torso's position and situation do not have to be corrected from the first moment. The method gets rid of a number of mistakes from the start. Thanks to

this method, the beginner sees the on guard position as easily doable and natural. The hands can be placed on the hips, but they can also be raised to the proper place and in the proper height immediately.

The weapon arm should be held with a loose shoulder, the elbow pulled in front of the waist (the elbow should be in front of the waist about a span), with a forearm that is pointing slightly upwards. The fingers can imitate the handle of a grip, with the thumbnail horizontal leaning outwards at a small angle.

The non-weapon arm should be lifted in a curve along the plane of the torso. The wrist should be at about the height of the face.

Today, the position of the non-weapon arm among competitors differs from the classical position in a number of ways. There are barely any fencers who hold their arms in a classical position. Many lift their elbows only up to the level of the waist. Formerly, the backward fling of the rear arm formerly helped the lunge and the retreat from it, based on the effect of the action-reaction principle. This phenomenon disappeared as the universal foil style changed and is probably not simply explained by laziness or love of comfort on the part of the fencers. The rear arm nowadays is only used for balance during footwork that is really fast and changes pace, position, and direction multiple times. Today, as soon as a student begins to fence bouts, he will unconsciously search for a more natural position for his hand and arm.

Nevertheless, a beginner fencer should be made to lift his non-weapon arm "properly" and use it during lunges and recoveries until the student becomes mature enough to be able to decide the question alone.

The classical position of the non-weapon arm developed after the period of two handed fencing and that is when it was incorporated into the technique. The partner originally used it to signal that he was fencing with one hand according to the new customs. The wide sleeves of the cloaks that fell from the lifted arm left the arm free. The partner could be sure that his opponent was not hiding a smaller dagger in the sleeve of his cloak, prepared for any opportunity which he could have stealthily exploited in a tight situation. Fencers wanted to avoid this by lifting their arms. This, a simple rule or gallant gesture, created out of caution, became a part of technique later on.

A number of exercises can be done in basic position and in on guard. Their purpose is to form the muscles and the joints in the image and likeness of fencing. A number of them can be used in the preparatory part of a Physical Education lesson as well. There are some that can be commanded like the classical gymnastic exercises. It is best if we have the students do these in their own rhythm.

It is advised to use the help of the bars or the assistance of a partner in the beginning of exercises connected to balance, so the fencer can achieve the formal requirements in addition to the practical ones. If in the beginning we commanded such exercises, we should allow the students later to execute them at their individual pace, so they can try to become used to the changes in cadence and rhythm, accelerating and decelerating, with exercises that are easier than fencing itself.

The exercises are strictly tied to forms. They only benefit a fencer if the person executes the exercises with the technical requirements in mind. It should be the coach's job to have the students understand this.

There are a number of variants of these exercises. On the one hand, we can preoccupy the students' attention with the variations, and on the other hand we can make the already known, practiced exercises more enjoyable.

The building blocks of footwork. Methods of gaining distance.

Footwork in fencing fills the role of infantry in warfare. One often has to attack or counterattack while in motion. Frequently the opponent can only be ambushed with the use of a complicated series of movements. In today's highly mobile fencing, which urges tempo from the feet and ignores the work of the blade, distance becomes the sole possibility for establishing contact. In light of the weight of this tendency, it is understandable why coaches stress footwork and the possibilities connected to it, such as mobility, springiness, lightness, looseness, or the enhancement of strength, explosiveness, stamina, pace, and the ability to change cadence and rhythm. The amalgamation of theseattributes transforms the fencer into a *motorized* infantry that can swiftly be sent to fight or be swiftly extracted.

The aim of footwork is *keeping the distance, advancing, gaining ground, changing situation or position, developing actions into hits, creating touches.*

Footwork is made up of steps, jumps, lunges, fleches, and the combinations of these. Combinations that are lighter or more explosive, or that vary in cadence and rhythm, provide solutions to bridge shorter-longer distances.

A *step* can be half, whole, classical, or cross-step.

Conscious half-steps are the tools of changing cadence and rhythm, and they are also exercises leading up to steps forward and backward, lunges, and the recovery from lunges. Half-steps also play a role as elements for gaining momentum in combinations. Half-steps with a sudden stop (check, stop-short) are the products of emergencies created by bouts.

The *classical steps* (feet following each other) are the foundation and the first step of teaching not only in foil, but all of the weapon types. The filling movement used for maneuvering today is also built on these types of steps.

Cross-steps are synonymous with normal walking. They make it possible to move continuously, distance one's self, and change the distance rapidly. Besides this, they are a pre-exercise for the fleche and the jump backward with legs crossing. Fencers suddenly made to jump often instinctively choose this type of step backward. The cross-step forward can be an antecedent to second intention or its accompanying phenomena.

The length of the classical steps, without breaks, can only be increased up to a certain limit. The length of the cross-steps can be larger immediately.

The body always moves instantly in case of cross-steps, while it is a bit more moderate in the case of classical steps. One must beware of starting with the upper body in the case of steps backward.

Classical steps can be *doubled* with a good rhythm. A more fluent series can be formed of cross-steps (the series can be infinite). The classical series steps are jerkier when going forward than backward.

Jumps are characterized by shorter or longer "flying" phases. Depending on which foot supplies the momentum necessary for the jump, the legs can cross or follow each other. One can only jump backward with crossed legs. Jumps started with the leg in the direction of the motion can be executed in both directions.

One usually gives a touch with a *lunge* at medium distance. The *fleche*, from long distance and upward, gives the possibility of hitting at longer distances.

From the point of view of function, we have:

- Footwork exercises with a role mainly or only in keeping the distance
- Footwork exercises playing a role in giving a touch

Steps and jumps are part of the populous first group. The second is represented by the lunge and fleche. Their separation in practice is not so stringent. Exceptions prove the rule, for example, when someone takes a step forward in close combat to close the distance and give a touch. The classical attacking combinations, step forward and lunge and the balestra also show the limitations of this separation.

Even though there are more and more fencers who pick the forward-backward jump (bounce), or jumping in place, as a means of preparation and gaining momentum, the steps forward and backward remain fundamental.

The technique and pedagogy of solo solutions, the types of mistakes, and the methods of correcting them.

1. *Step forward.* Its variations:
    a.) Starting with the front foot (Fig. 13).

The front foot lifts and reaches, toes near the ground, then rolls onto the ground, touching first with the heel at a distance according to the size of the intended step. (Landing the foot on the heel can be the first phase of the exercise when it is broken into parts). Meanwhile the freed energy from the rear leg pushes the body, which is already in motion, and follows it quickly, fixing the size of the step. The order in which the parts of the rear foot touch the ground has to be barely visible, first done by the pads and then the rest of the sole.

It is advisable to make the first steps shorter than the so-called classical one-foot length, in order for the phases to be united better. We should move on to longer steps later. When teaching, we should strive for the end of the steps to be faster. Later we can vary this for tactical reasons.

At first, both legs should take the same size steps so the fencer can learn the step forward in a technically correct manner. Although this cannot always be required later, a

Figure 13

beginner should be taught this way in order to maintain good rhythm and balance.

The average length of the step is just one-half to three-quarters of the fencer's foot. Taking a larger step within a critical distance can only be done with the danger of receiving a tempo (stop thrust). The fencer spends more time in the air, unable to act, in an unstable balance position, on one foot. During longer steps, the work of the two feet becomes different to a larger extent.

The amount of toe lift always depends on the size of the step. Momentum is more stressful with wide steps, it is less stressful during short steps, but it still exists even with the shortest steps, even if the fencer is able to start the steps from the classical stance. If he is not, then just as with every footwork exercise, this is governed by the rules of the given situation. If the body weight is based on the front foot, it becomes impossible to start a step by lifting the toes. In such a case, one can only start the step by lifting the knee.

The first half of a step forward, under ideal circumstances, is similar to normal human walking, when the swinging foot has passed the vertical line. The situation of "toes up and heel down" – that is, the pointing position of the foot, and the touching of the ground with the heel first during a step – can be experienced while walking.

The step forward must be finished quickly with the rear foot, which must stay close to the ground. (Putting the foot down must be faster than lifting it.)

We take shorter steps in high on guard positions and longer steps in deeper positions. Distance can be closely adjusted with tiny, stamping steps. The middle steps used for keeping the distance are longer (it is advisable to keep changing the size of the steps so it will not be easy for the opponent to get on to the fencer, adapt to him, get used to him), but the steps should rarely exceed the size of the length of a foot.

Depending on its purpose, footwork can have soft, careful, stealthy, exploratory traits or it can be open, uncovered, determined, fast, and with first intention.

If we consider the step a simple exercise, the students can copy our demonstrations, containing verbal instructions as well. A good rhythm, with short steps, can soon be brought out of the students. In order to work on the details (since those do not develop on their own) and in order to correct the mistakes as they appear, one should rely on appropriate exercises that have specific aims, the ones which lead up to a required movement, as well as methods that help the execution of a given exercise. The details should be corrected in the order of importance or chronology.

Since no absolute method exists (not even dividing the movements into parts, though some would claim this), the drawbacks of each method must be remedied with another method. It seems to be a better solution if a coach does not strictly cling to one method; that is, he should mix the methods at hand, choosing them, switching them, using them one after the other.

Mistakes in the step forward

- Starting by lifting the knee. This can be corrected by having the foot and toes lifted before the leg starting the movement.

- Dragging the rear foot on the ground at the end of the step. This can be corrected if we have the step forward done over a weapon placed on the ground between the two feet (closer to the rear foot). (The blade must be stepped over near the point, in order to avoid breaking the blade if the student accidentally steps on it.)

- Advancing late and languidly with the rear foot. We can speed this up by moving the rear leg along a higher arc, placing it on the ground strongly and with a sound. This phase can be separated from the step as a whole and it can be practiced in place in on guard with loosely extended legs. (The student should sit into the on guard when the foot touches the ground.)

b) *Starting with the rear foot (inverse step forward)*

We place the rear foot behind the heel of the front foot and we have the on guard position taken up again with the front foot. This method allows for a careful approach.

The first half of the step is common in combinations. It is a simple method for gaining distance, as long as it is followed by a lunge or a fleche.

Since this is not an exercise intended for beginners (they often take such steps instinctively, messing up the correct order, committing mistakes while learning the classical step), after a short verbal command, a few hints and demonstrations are usually enough for the right execution of the exercise. It mostly becomes a part of one's repertoire during a bout.

c.) *Cross-steps forward*

This is the most natural footwork exercise. Therefore it is enough to tell the ones interested in it which leg starts the step and on which side it overtakes and crosses the other leg.

From on guard, the rear leg crosses the foot remaining on the ground (the stepping foot usually touches the ground at the middle of the motionless foot) and then the other foot crosses *behind* the previous foot to arrive in on guard once again.

During cross-steps the weapon arm can act more freely. It becomes more fluent to execute a fleche from this type of step. Teaching it is less problematic, due to its natural quality.

2.   STEP BACKWARD. Its variations:

a.) *Starting with the rear foot*

The rear foot stretches backward, flat and close to the ground. (This first phase should already move the torso, the upper body.) At the same time, the front leg pushes the body backward with a rising foot; then, before extending the knee completely, the front foot leaves the ground and follows the other one, finally touching the ground and finishing the step. For the step backward, the same rules apply as for the step forward regarding the length of the steps, the unity of phases, and the comparison of speed. (One must be faster during the second half of the step here as well, so the fencer will not remain too long in an unbalanced and vulnerable position.)

Two typical mistakes of the classical step backward occur when the student leaves his torso behind or leans forward with it at the beginning of the step. The coach or a partner can correct this with the hand by gently pushing the front shoulder at the launch of the movement, indicating for the torso, too, to move immediately.

Even those who are fans of breaking exercises into sequences do not split the step backward into two parts. Focusing on the first phase would be more of an unnatural situation than anything so far and one could not execute the end correctly.

b.) Starting with the front foot (inverse step backward)

With the front foot of the on guard position we step in front of the heel of the foot in the rear and then we take a step backward with the latter foot to take up the on guard position once again.

It is a rare type of step. The first half is a unique way of defending against hits aimed at the leg in epee. It can be used to create discord and to win phases. Students should only practice it on their own, once they have practiced the classical steps, so stepping with differing legs will not confuse beginners. If there is a need for its use (combination of footwork exercises), a short description and a few demonstrations are usually enough for advanced fencers to execute it correctly.

c.) Cross-steps backward (Fig. 14)

The front foot crosses the rear foot behind the heel. (Usually the toes of the stepping foot and the heel of the motionless foot end up on the same line.) Then the other foot takes its step, uncrossing the legs and resuming the on guard position.

Generally those people who retreat because of reflexes, those who see distance as a form of defense are the ones who use this variation. Those who are attacked suddenly not only take the step, they might also jump this type of step. They basically do a reflex-like jump backward with this. The dynamics, understandably, are weaker in this case than during a direct jump backward.

Students learn the backward cross-step quickly since it is a natural type of step.

Footwork must be taught by beginning with the classical steps forward and backward. Besides the general methods, other methods can help the coach concerning this topic.

For example:
- Combine the first half of step backward and the second half of step forward and practice this prior to the actual full steps.
- Another solution is to stand in front of a line of students who are in on guard and make them step in place. Use your movements to make them step backward and forward, but be sure to say the direction of the movement. After a short while, the movement of the coach's body will be enough to

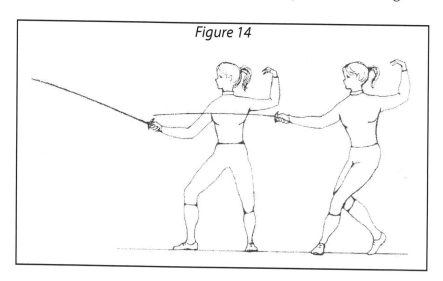

Figure 14

control the students, so they will be accustomed to the sight of live signals and responding to them with logical responses as soon as possible. Nevertheless, we should always verbally communicate the most important criteria regarding the technique.

As a fun and competitive form of the exercise, the students can respond to the commands with the opposite direction and frequency (one step instead of two, two steps instead of one, retreating instead of advancing and advancing instead of retreating). The coach chooses the pace of the dictation. The ones who miss the direction or the frequency receive a symbolic hit. Tightening the space between the students pushes them to pay closer attention, if they wish to avoid the mistakes committed by their neighbors.

The two methods above, just as for the whole of methodology, can be one of the roads leading to Rome.

3. *Lunge.* Its variations:
    a.) Forward lunge (Figs. 15, 16, 17)

We should start the lunge like starting the step forward, except that the start is more vehement. The first graspable sign should be the lifting the foot and the toes. At the same time the leg should swing strongly toward the opponent like a pendulum. This first movement, which frees the leg from strain, sets the body in motion, and provides a place and possibility for the lunge, must be followed without delay by the work of the rear leg that drives the point to the target.

The knee of the rear leg must already be extended before the heel of the front foot touches the ground, after which the fencer rolls onto his sole. (The length of the lunge is always defined by the distance between the two feet once the movement has ended and not the distance that the fencer moves by flying in the air or by sliding on the ground once he has arrived in the lunge position.)   97

Figure 15

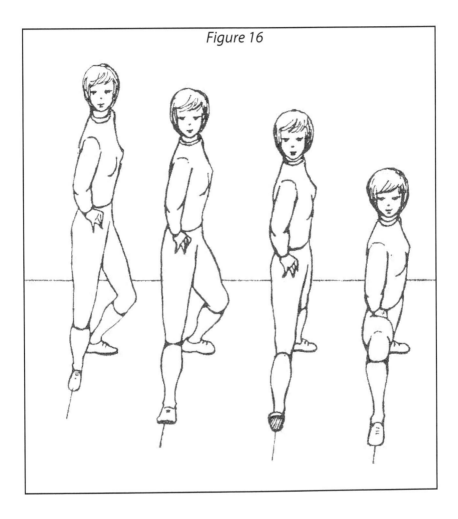

Figure 16

Figure 17

The heel of the front foot should be moving towards its aim flat and close to the ground. This can only be done if the knee of the front foot is above the ankle in the beginning. If for some reason it is ahead of the ankle, the fencer will only be able to move his shin by lifting his knee, because in this case the distance between the knee and the ground is shorter than the length of the shin.

The front foot takes part in the execution of the lunge more or less forcefully, depending on the intention of the fencer. Sometimes it simply reaches ahead like during a step, other times it forcefully swings ahead taking the body with it, forcing the rear leg to work faster as well.

From the on guard position, the rear leg acts like a compressed spring during the lunge. It can work its effect instantaneously, that is to say explosively, (one has to be born with this) or with an accelerating characteristic (one can learn this). Depending on whether the fencer releases the spring suddenly or gradually, we can talk about the pressing, pushing, or shoving work of the rear leg.

Lunges that are short, restrained, and less dynamic (the rear leg should be extended only moderately) are used for reconnaissance, false attacks, second intentions, and methods of gaining distance. The ones that are striving to hit with first intention are wide and have an elemental force. The full strength and length of the rear leg must be used in this case.

The first half of a correct lunge is flatter and longer, the descending part is shorter, more curved, and steeper. A lunge that reaches too high in its first phase puts extra weight on the front leg when landing, so that the fencer needs more power to hold the body back, and to stop its forward and downward motion.

Once the knee of the rear leg is extended (the sole should stay on the ground) the heel of the front foot must touch the ground. Then the fencer bends his knee and rolls onto the sole of the front foot, stabilizing the end position. The muscles of the thigh work as shock absorbers in this last phase.

The rear leg must be extended one moment before the

heel of the lunging foot touches the ground. If the order is switched, the follow-up extension of the rear leg will not change the size of the lunge. It will, however, push the body onto the front foot, thus increasing its strain. An incorrect end position is a bad omen for a retreat.

The longer a lunge is, the more difficult it becomes to stop in it, to hold in the last moment during the final stage, to limit it, stay standing in the lunge, parry in it, or retreat from it.

The length of the lunge is influenced by the looseness of the waist, natural or acquired (adequate exercises are necessary for this), the ratio of the torso, the legs, the thigh, and the shins, and the strength of the thighs.

Only with great amounts of power can one maintain the original position of the torso in a maximal lunge with a large spread. It is useless to force this. One has to strive for this momentum not to over step the acceptable size. That is, the attacker should remain the master of his own movements.

If the fencer artificially pushes his torso forward to compensate for short stretching ability, the rear hip is inevitably raised. This can make the handling of the weapon become unstable.

The lunge finishes in its characteristic position. In the technically acceptable longest lunge, the front shin is vertical, while the thigh is horizontal. If we place our front foot ahead too much, the norms of the end positions will not be acquired: the lunge will be like a forward split.

The knee of the rear foot must be parallel to the ground facing sideways in the end position. If it turns towards the ground, it will turn the foot and the ankle joint on to its inner sole. The gripping surface of the sole –which the fencer may need in order to recover to guard – is largely lost.

The knee of the front leg bends inwards in a lunge to a smaller-larger extent. (This also depends on the length of the lunge.) This is more emphatic for those with wider waists. It can be fixed through lots of work and fatigue. Nevertheless, it is better to have the front knee bend inwards than to have the back knee turn towards the ground. That is not only incorrect technically, it also damages the knee.

d.) Backward lunge

This is not used as a footwork exercise in live fencing; one cannot win space with it, only the center of gravity ends up deeper than in the on guard. It is useful, however, for relaxing the hip joint, whether the fencer reaches the ominous end position at once, with one movement of the rear leg, or by inching towards it by lifting, turning the heel and foot alternately backward until reaching it. (The torso should stay straight all along.) Beginners and children can use the help of the bars or their partners if necessary during the initial attempts. The exercise can be done the opposite way as well. The best execution is the one by inching; it is a better and more effective exercise for loosening the hip, than by springing on the front leg in a lunge.

4. *Recovery from lunge.* Its variations:

a.) Recovering backward (Fig. 18)

From the lunge, the torso is moved from its stable condition by the thrust resulting from the emphatic push of the front foot. The pulling strength of the rear leg gradually increases because the angle between the thigh and the shin is decreasing as they approach the body. Before the pushing effect is over, the fencer pushes himself from the ground somewhat. From then on only the rear foot is working. It can cooperate more efficiently if the knee bends slantwise upwards. The heel of the front foot should make contact with the ground. If the fencer used his non-weapon arm for the lunge, he can use its reverse action once again. (Flinging the arm heightens the pushing power forward and the pulling power backward.)

We use the backward recovery to return to the on guard position from a lunge.

The lunge and the recovery backward from it are the types of footwork exercises containing the most serious and largest possibilities of mistakes. It is especially difficult to combine the pushing-pulling and pulling-pushing work of the legs. A number of problems can be avoided as long as the coach:

- *Teaches the lunge as a position first.* Setting up the position can be the following: the students stand in a side straddle with the feet parallel, two and a half foot lengths apart. Following this, right-handed fencers bend their right knee; left-handed ones bend their left knee; then turn their lead feet, knees, and heads according to the given direction.
- *Teaches beginners the method of recovering backward to the on guard position first.* Two exercises can be helpful in this.
  - Practicing, from a shortened lunge position, the extending-pushing movement of the lifted front foot of the lunge synchronized with the back knee's active pulling movement, bending back and forth multiple times.
  - The other exercise is for gripping the ground with the heel of the front foot, practiced by doing recoveries from short lunges, first without placing the sole on the ground, instead simply placing the heel on it.
- Finally, *if the coach gradually increases the length of the lunges proportionally to the adapting abilities of the muscles and joints,* the fencer also learns by this that he does not always have to do the longest lunge. (The shorter a lunge is, the less extension is required from the rear leg.)

b) Radoppio (forward recovery from the lunge)
We use the forward recovery (moving the rear leg for-

Figure 18

ward) in cases when we want to close the distance, renew attacks, or follow a retreating opponent. Evidently, a lunge cannot be as long in such instances as a lunge intended for hitting in a direct attack.

It is one of the easiest exercises to execute. The heel of the extended rear leg is lifted first. Then it steps forward to take up the on guard position by pushing the body off the ground with the ball of the foot. (Meanwhile the torso is slightly bent forward; the body weight is based on the front leg.)

The longer a lunge, the shorter our step forward, the shorter a lunge, the longer our step forward can be, sometimes almost shrinking the new on guard into a basic position.

It is worth mentioning when this movement should be taught. If it is being taught too early, one can fear that the students will choose this type of recovery, whether necessary or not, instead of the more difficult, yet much more useful and frequent type of recovery.

5. THE JUMP FORWARD

While the rear foot remains motionless, the front foot reaches forward flat above the ground then hits the ground as quickly as it started, with almost horizontal soles. As soon as the front foot starts its downward motion, the fencer jumps forward from his rear leg, without releasing the "springs" from it. Following this, after arranging the feet in the air, he lands in the on guard again. The two feet must land on the ground at the same time.

To execute the exercise correctly, it is easier for the fencer to practice the movement of the front leg, without jumping anywhere, stamping on the ground with his sole, and then trying to practice the jump of the rear leg separately, and then only afterwards moving on to the combination of the different work of the two feet. It also helps to do the first attempts from a narrower on guard position where the center of gravity is higher.

The dynamic type of jump forward is used to push the opponent to counterattack or as a first intention attack if combined with a lunge. The jumps used for preparation are soft and light; they usually barely gain space; they have a more of a signaling value.

6. *THE JUMP BACKWARD.* Its variations:
    a.) Starting with the rear foot

Its technique is the opposite of the jump forward; it is a stylized variation of the shot-putter's footwork. The rear foot should not be lifted too much during the backward reach. The movement will bend the torso forward a bit. This is a natural accompaniment of this technique.

After a few preliminary rear-foot reaches and ground touches (the foot should hit the ground), the jump will not create any problems.

The work of the rear foot is emphasized during a long jump backward, and each foot begins its movement at a different time. During short jumps, the beginning is more of a signal, the two feet follow each other faster, and during skipping-like jumps they leave the ground almost simultaneously.

    b.) Starting with the front foot
      1. By crossing the legs

The center of gravity is pushed onto the back leg by a strong backward reach of the front leg, from which the fencer jumps off. (The size of the reach depends on the dynamics of the start and the planned length of the jump.) Preparation for arresting the large momentum of the body must be started while the fencer is in the air, by rearranging the legs into on guard position. The longer and higher the curve of a jump, the harder and more difficult will the landing be. The flying phase ends with the feet hitting the ground.

No matter how the fencers try to round off the execution, the jump backward executed by crossing the legs will always be a bit chunky and square. That is why today's competitor willingly chooses the other type of jump, which offers more possibilities for continuing the action. They will only jump with crossed legs if they are absolutely sure that the opponent will not follow them or if the continuity of the bout, for some reason, is broken for a shorter-longer period of time.

We gradually increase the length of the jump when teaching it.

The simplest method of teaching it is if, as a synonym, we refer to the cross-step backward. The student will jump this alone as it is done faster and faster.

2. Without crossing the legs

The legs do not necessarily have to cross each other in jumps backward started with the front leg. This only happens during jumps intended for longer distance. Here, the front leg often only approaches the one on the ground. With this execution, the jump can be softer and lighter. The feet follow each other with minimal differences when landing on the ground.

7. THE FLECHE

The fleche is an efficient way of hitting. However, it has an all-or-nothing quality that requires more careful preparation than an attack made with a lunge.

The hit should arrive when the big toe of the rear foot is still on the ground. The fencer's body, his arm, and the weapon have to span between these two points. Depending on the dynamics, the distance, and the abilities of the fencer, the angle between the fencer's body and the ground should usually be between 45^0 and 60^0. The fleche is correct if the substantive part of the footwork is finished when the hit happens. Following this, we can only talk of "running out," holding down the momentum.

a.) Execution from on guard (Figs. 19, 20)

The movement should be started by an extension of the weapon arm in the proper height and direction, enhanced by pushing the back hip down. The rear leg pushes the up-

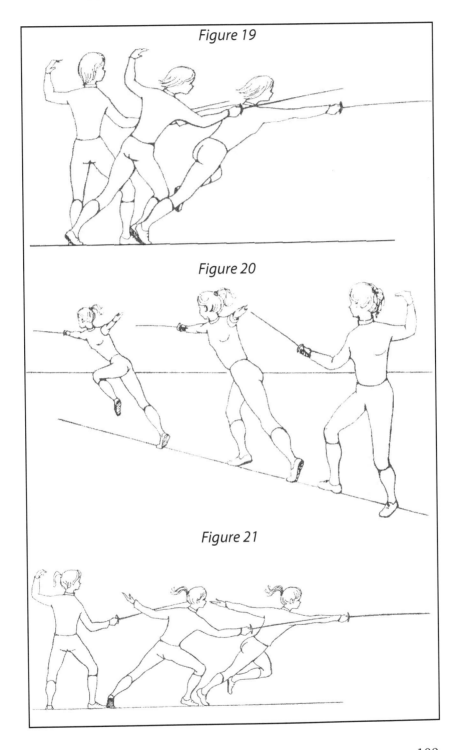

Figure 19

Figure 20

Figure 21

per body forward to the verge of losing balance and gradually pushes the body weight onto the front leg until the rear leg leaves the ground, with a lifted knee, crossing the front leg in the air. After this only the front foot has a say in the fate of the fleche, accepting the lion's share of the explosive execution.

b.) Execution in various ways from a lunge to continue the action

1. The fencer takes a step forward with the rear foot.
2. The fencer takes a step backward with the front foot.
3. The fencer steps with both feet. The front foot goes backward and the rear foot steps forward in order to create the perfect position for a fleche.
4. Moving with both feet at the same time between the on guard position and a lunge
5. The foot of the extended leg starts the attack with a pushing movement (Fig. 21). This last version is usually worth doing in case of lunges made on short distances.

Footwork combinations.

We rarely meet solo footwork exercises in live fencing. They are ranged into rows based on the rate of their convertibility, pro and contra.

Footwork for maneuvering consists of a practical combination of movements. It is impossible to make rules for their associations. The fight for distance and fencing bouts with multiple steps require the longest combinations.

The demand, necessity or compulsion, the applied method, the form, the degree of affinity, the clash between the offensive-defensive intents, the distance, and finally the pace of the bout all influence the possibility of tighter-looser linkages between footwork movements.

The combinations are made up of partially opportunistic and partially teachable associations. The variations, ready to follow each other in rapid sequence, are returning moments, frequent characters, and intentionally used blocks of footwork. Teaching them should be begun after teaching the solo footwork exercises.

Characteristic footwork associations

6. *Step forward – lunge.*

Its significant marks are its rhythm form, which can be written out like a tune, and its accelerating tendency. These marks not only make it recognizable; they enable the phases to be separated one by one. The "classical" syncopated step forward does not enable the seamless melding of the parts; therefore the feet land simultaneously at the end of the step forward and the front foot releases almost simultaneously to start the lunge. This fast lift-off from the ground reduces and compresses the step forward – lunge, originally made up of three cadences, into two, through benign cheating.

The rear foot finishes the step with resounding force. This naturally accompanies the footwork of direct actions launched with great élan and designed to hit in one tempo. The speed and not the force should make the sound. This lags behind during careful, second intention advances. The foot, nevertheless, must be lifted in such cases as well.

7. *Double step forward.*

Its rhythm should be exactly the same as for the step forward – lunge. Thus it can be an exercise leading up to that.

8. *Double step backward.*

This will not have the unalloyed rhythmic harmony of its opposite direction partner, no matter how hard one tries.

The second, faster step should hardly be longer than the shortened first step, which is not longer than a medium length in any case.

9. Step forward – step backward.
Rhythm marks the steps here. The fencer should try to make a short, fast step forward, followed by a longer, easy step backward. It is a useful tool for breaking the distance.

10. Step backward – step forward.
This combination is provided by the short, appel-like, rhythmic step backward.

11. The balestra (jump forward lunge).
Although it is not as frequent as the step forward – lunge, it is still a characteristic combat combination. Due to its dynamics, it is a customary attendant of actions combined with beats.

If we shorten the jump and decrease the strain on the front leg in the air, in order to start the lunge, the fit will be perfect. Continuity suffers with longer jumps.

The step forward – lunge has a gradual speed; the balestra has a more vehement beginning. Although their top speed is about the same (there are or can be differences based on the individual), the balestra is btter suited the explosive, short or short-legged, strong-muscled fencers better. Taller fencers and ones with longer arms and legs readily choose the advantages of the step forward – lunge.

12. Jump forward – step backward.
The body weight should move forward by the end of the jump, so the rear leg can start the retreat straight away, once it touches the ground.

13. Jump forward – step forward.
The jump is more of a signal (advance and winning space hardly happens), so the step can be done without delay. The

not so dynamic jump is followed by a longer, lazier step.

14. Slide (glide).

This is nothing more than the first half of a step forward partnered with an immediate flat, skipping-like jump executed with both feet, in the same direction. Landing on the ground should happen at about the same time with both feet.

15. Standstill (stop-short or check).

The fencer takes a short step forward, then slides the front foot forward again as in the *slide*. Then the fencer presses the foot into the ground without finishing the step forward and steps backward.

16. Combinations with the fleche.

The fleche can be perfectly combined with half-steps and beginning of steps. The variations of these:

a.) The fleche is executed immediately after the first half of the classical step forward. Stepping with a bent upper body is an important requirement – not a mistake.

b.) We close the rear foot, in a quick cadence, tightly behind the heel of the front foot. Meanwhile the replacement of the body weight takes place, so the fleche can be started as soon as possible.

c.) The competitor closes his feet with a step backward, started with the front foot. The arm is meanwhile extended, and the upper body bends forward, so the fleche can be started. The half-step backward should be with a quick cadence so the fencer can lean on it when the fleche starts.

These are the combination pairs that are practiced during training as well.

More than two footwork exercises can be connected during teaching. We usually do not practice exercises with more than three combinations. The others are brought forth from a fencer by practice.

It is worth practicing only practical combinations; far-fetched ones should be avoided. It is not worth doing those even if they are aimed for developing "skills." (An example of this would be combining a jump forward with a jump backward started with the rear foot.)

During bouts, the elements of footwork, repeated out of reflex, should be combined in a good rhythm. These cominations have to be preferred during teaching.

At least in foil and epee, the balestra, the jumpforward – step backward, and even the jump forward itself, are footwork exercises on the verge of extinction, so much so that in the near future it will not even be worth considering them as special exercises for developing skills.

Footwork and distance

Distance is a consideration in every substantive act and intention aimed to give a hit or avoid one. It affects footwork, the coordination of the arm and the feet, and the time during which the given action is executed. It colors the work with the weapon. It influences the position of the parries, their closeness to the body, and their frontal trait. It also affects the place and method of hitting.

Fencers aim to keep each other at a respectful distance during the time of preparation, reconnaissance, and getting a feel for the opponent's style. (Distance is a tool of passive defense.) The intention changes with time. One of the competitors breaks the distance because of his planned action. The turn of the balance usually benefits the initiating person.

The audience first sees this struggle for distance made up of maneuvers in opposite directions, foreshadowings, and intentions. (This part of the bout is spectacular and can be easily followed.) The shorter opponent has a more difficult job in the combat with changing luck and varying roles (the fencer can be the dictator or the follower). He must stand farther away if he wants to be in safety; he must go closer if he wishes to hit. The size of the critical distance is measured in millimeters. The late Dr. László Duronelly, former teacher of the Hungarian National College of Physical Education, aptly refers to this with his statement: "A good fencer is always close enough to hit his opponent, yet somehow always too far away to be hit."

The maneuvering, filling movements, which make up a considerable part of the bout, can be aimed at keeping or breaking the distance. Keeping the distance happens with synchronic movement, following or answering the dictated footwork similarly; while breaking it can happen by obstructing the dictated footwork with reciprocal moves, frustrating the opponent's intention to adjust and adapt, and by changing the components of time, space, and dynamics. Good fencers can do this in the role of follower as well. The surprise is bigger; the success is more certain, if the fencer strives for winning distance from a supposed passivity.

Flat, monotonous footwork helps both the job of the person keeping the distance and that of the person trying to break it – for example, the mechanical repetition of footwork exercises (e.g., always taking two steps forward and one step back), or of regular rhythmic features that can be written out like a tune (e.g., two fast steps followed by one slow step). The form, the direction, the erratic character of the pace, the uncertainty arising out of this, the continuously vibrating, changing image all make the opponent's task more difficult.

Keeping the distance should be practiced first. Once the students have learned the steps forward and backward, the coach should pair them up. He should point out the dictating person or line, and he should make the other students fill the adjusting role first slowly, then in a quicker pace. The fencers can hold each other's hands as a way of helping. They can have their palms touching with extended or bent arms, or they can press a glove or a mask together with the open palms facing their opponent. (The dropping of these items signals a mistake.) In case of bent arms, the original angle of the lower and upper arm cannot change. The fencer cannot compensate for the incorrect distance by stretching or bending the arm further during motion.

Footwork must be connected with the work of the blade in time. This activity, which is a part of success and helps camouflage and concealment, can be made up of engagements, binds, changes of engagement-binds, beats, combinations of bind-beats or beat-binds, the extension of the blade and the arm to different extents and speeds, or the opposite way, recovering the arm from a line. This should be followed by practicing the ways of gaining distance.

If a fencer has fast legs, gradually, continuously accelerated steps forward can help the fencer reach his opponent who is keeping the distance. This method of gaining distance is effective when the footwork is revved up without any signs of intention, following a soothing, soft, slow phase of pushing and pulling. We can finish our attacking intention with a lunge, fleche or step forward – lunge, or a step forward – fleche as the last move.

We can close the distance by suddenly halting after the use of footwork with quick cadence. The standstill can cause disruption, a delay in the ability of adjusting; we are already standing while the opponent in motion is still taking a step. This can give an advantage for the person trying to hit, who can be assisted in exploiting the situation by the short period of hesitation and perplexity.

The synchronized movement, the harmony can be broken if our repeated maneuvering filling movement based on back and forth steps is suddenly changed to jump forward – step forward, double steps forward, sliding the foot, or coming to a sudden standstill. Thanks to stealing the cadence, we can win space against ambush as well. We can elude, break away from, even those who follow and adjust to our movement perfectly if these footwork exercises are followed by a strongly slowed step backward. The reason is that during this slow step backward, there is scarcely any distance opening. (With a normal step backward we would increase the distance from the already broken off opponent.)

Breaking the distance, when begun from a retreat or with a step backward is a more difficult exercise and our aim as the follower or adjusting partner is to steal the cadence sooner, than would our dictating opponent. This is how we do it: we only *begin* one of our steps backward – that is, take a quarter, maximum half step, or start the step backward with the front foot, from which we immediately attack. It is important for us to react to the opponent's preparatory movements with deeper steps. We lure him closer with this, which can be an advantageous occasion for executing our action.

In a desperae fight, in tense moments during a bout close to a loss, or when someone has a major time, touch, or space disadvantage, e.g. standing on the back line, sometimes even the simplest tricks can disrupt an opponent who is not able to control his reflexes, in judging the distance. Stretching or bending the weapon arm in a larger degree, combining it with the same or opposite direction of footwork can create a misleading sense of proper distance in the eyes of the attacked person when the attacker is already close.

It is often enough to take a half step forward in an emphasized, deeper position (we thus evoke a full step backward from the opponent). As soon as we sense his distance opening movement, the beginning of his reacting move, we should start the retreat of the front foot into on guard without delay. When our opponent throws himself forward to recreate the original distance, we should attack him with a lunge. The recovery back to the on guard – the move aimed at pulling – should be accompanied by a rise of our center of gravity. Our pushing-pulling intent will be made more effective by an emphasized sitting down and rising.

One should rely on more difficult forms of breaking the distance against opponents with routine. (The prerequisite for their use is the full knowledge of the footwork variants. They should be tried individually, before a paired exercise or the bout.) A type of this is when we only signal a step forward with our front foot, but we step right behind the front heel with our rear foot, without significantly raising our center of gravity. We win a distance of about up to two steps forward in the time of one cadence, while our opponent only opens the distance to the size of one step. Since he did not notice the loss of distance, he feels safe. We, on the other hand, can launch a successful attack from a shorter distance.

V. Foil Fencing: History and Basic Concepts

The foil as we now know it was born in the middle of the eighteenth century and it entered history as the practice weapon for the smallsword. The first rule was to prohibit thrusts against the head (the prohibition of these, of course, was not valid for actual combat), since the masks used at that time did not provide perfect protection: they were made of leather, with a narrow slit for the eyes. People often rejected their use during practice due to their weight. This resulted in a number of accidents and deaths. At the same time, stuffed fencing jackets, thickly padded, were used for protecting the body.

The beginning of fencing as a sport goes back to about 1750, when the invention of the wire woven mask around 1750 lifted the ban on some actions and alowed for more speed at the same time. The competitors did not have to hold themselves back and could perform most actions with total élan.

Since competitions were fought with the foils, it became the classical weapon of the sport. These competitions were more of an academic demonstration by two fencers, rather than competitions in today's sense. These were some of the methods, before the modern sport, for promoting fencing, introducing its beauty, vigor, and values, hinting towards the future. It was not uncommon for the audience to work with the judges to decide touches; they also honored elegant solutions when deciding on a winner.

Foil remained the basic weapon type for a long time, since it was believed that precise handling of a weapon could only be learned with the foil. Almost everyone, even sabreurs, began with foil and switched to their preferred weapon only later. This period, here in Hungary, lasted until the middle or end of the 1940s. Afterwards this opinion only constrained epee fencers, since many coaches still believed that foil was a necessary prerequisite of epee. Today, epee fencers are trained without foil basics.

At first, foil was fenced with a dry (non-electric) blade in front of a human jury consisting of a director and four side judges. The foil machine, the scoring apparatus, the electric weapon were systematically introduced in 1955.

The early electric foil had a clumsy weight distribution, resulting at first in a decrease in technique because the point was heavy, the blade was whippy, and the use of the pistol grip led to wide actions. The point dragged on the blade and often arrived later than the blade, resulting in attempted thrusts hitting with the side of the blade. This especially affected ripostes, so as soon as competitors observed this problem, they began using repeated remises. Foil almost became a second epee. Many thought of shortening the blade once they saw this situation; others believed it was unnecessary to have two combat-like weapon types in one sport.

Foil was finally saved by the production of slimmer, lighter, and shorter points. This reduced the drag on the blade, which was bad for fencing and dangerous as well. (However, anyone who watches a slow-motion video can see how much whippiness remains!)

Thanks to the electric weapon and the scoring machine, it now became possible to aim for parts of the valid target that existed only in theory during the period of dry foil fencing because the jury could not see them. The fencer of the previous era had to allow for the jury's limitations. To award a touch, the point had to be seen to hit and blade had to be seen to bend. This is no longer the case. It is enough for the point to exert a pressure of 500 grams for the light to turn on.

Only touches hitting the valid target surface count (this is covered by a conductive surface on competitions fenced with signaling machines). The head and the limbs do not count as valid targets. The valid touches are signaled by a colored light (red or green) while white lights signal the invalid touches. As the lights turn on, a sound signal is heard as well.

The torso in theory can be hit anywhere. In practice however, it is usually attacked on the side of the weapon arm, toward the middle of the chest. (This partially depends on the difference between the heights of the fencers.) We less often hit below this, under the side of the weapon arm (flank), the shoulder blade of the weapon arm, or the deep target on the side of the non-weapon arm.

We generally target *areas* that give us a goodangle for hitting. However, we must target pints on covered or partially covered surfaces where the angle is disadvantageous.

Thrusts will likely be spread out to a smaller-larger extent around the point that is targeted during practice. The attacker is excited because of the stakes or makes technical errors; the opponent is moving and shifting his body. The target comes closer, then it's far away again; the point must be directed against a moving body. This spread, however, cannot be too big because the target area is relatively small.

Comparing the dry and electric foil. The foil grip.

Today's pistol grip electric foil is not as well-balanced as the dry foil with a French or Italian grip. The dry foil could be balanced one or two finger's widths from the guard. Today, the balance point of even the best pistol grip electric foils is at a distance of 4-5 fingers. The lighter pommel nut, which is situated in the middle of the pistol grip and not at its end, is a major factor. The large French pommel was a good counterweight at the end of the long grip. The balance point of the Italian foil, despite a shorter grip and a lighter, slimmer pommel, was also closer to the hilt because of the heavier crossbar. The heavier point is also a factor. Thus the electric foil remains point-heavy, even though points today are half as big as their precursors.

However, the swing, the inertia, the pull, and the delay of the point (which follows its own path) are actually necessary in some actions and must be considered in complex actions. (Fencers use this characteristic in part, when they want to get to covered or partially covered regions.) The greater weight, the heavier blade, and the "lazier" point all have to be calculated in the work of the hand, arm, and weapon.

Shorter, lighter weapons are produced with better distribution of the weight and with slimmer grips for younger fencers, since they cannot hold or benefit from the use of a normal weight and sized weapon.

Nowadays, the so-called pistol or revolver grip is used for teaching and competing around the world (Fig. 22). Students whose coach believes that it is more advantageous to use a straight grip in the initial period when learning the technique, begin with French grip only (Fig. 23). With time, however, they switch to the pistol grip as well. Today the Italian grip and guard with its crossbar is only a curiosity of fencing history.

There are several pistol grip designs. Some have print-like bulges marking the place of the fingers. On others the projec-

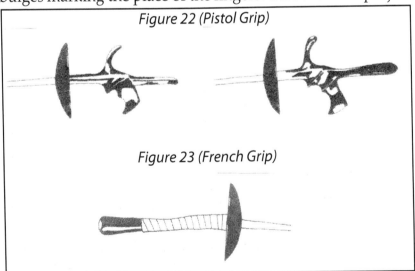

Figure 22 (Pistol Grip)

Figure 23 (French Grip)

tions are deeper. Some offer a steeper place for the middle, the ring and the little finger, so the fingers are above each other; while offer a downward-diagonal position where the fingers are behind one another. The thickness of the front part also varies: it may be slightly curved or flat and squared. Last, but not least, comes the prong, starting from the front part and leading to the base of the thumb and index finger. This prong may be pointing up or slightly down, curved or straight, longer or shorter, thinner or thicker. This latter feature decides whether the thumb and the index finger can be situated above each other when holding the weapon, or if the thumb is pushed towards the inner side of the grip into a bad position and disadvantageous angle. This affects handling the weapon to a great extent.

The choice of a grip depends on its configuration, its weight, the length of its front part, the direction and angles of its indentations, prongs or bulges, and whether they are following each other loosely or tightly. All of these must be suited to the size of the fencer's palm, hand, and fingers. Ideally, the grip would be molded to the fencer's hand. As it is, one must select among the manufactured grips. In the beginning, the coach has to help with this; in the end, the fencer has to make the choice.

The thumb and the index finger straddle the grip from underneath and above, facing each other and being opposed (if there is already a curve of the blade it should bend downward from the guard; the groove where the wire is placed should look up). The first joint of the slightly bent thumb will be above the meeting point of the first and second joints of the index finger. (These two fingers can slightly touch the foil pad.) The middle, the ring, and the pinkie fingers are placed on the side of the static grip in the furrow of the palm (Fig. 24). Their places are already given by the configuration on the pistol grip. Since there are no such bases on the French grip, the fingers have to be positioned by the fencer. (The fingers should be situated loosely behind each other; the little finger should also hold the grip.)

All of the fingers take part in handling the weapon, without any strict separation regarding the roles. The ones closer to the guard take part in leading, directing the point and launching it. The ones in the back are entrusted with the power with which the blade is wielded; they have a greater role in making the grip stronger, and preventing its motions from becoming too big.

Some grips are cut short, placing the middle, the ring, and the little finger vertically above each other (instead of behind). These give a narrow grip, thus limiting the free movement of the fingers. Those who use such weapons often unconsciously help themselves by allowing the wrist to work more. The wrist thus takes the leading, rather than a supporting role. This is seen to some extent in almost all beginners.

A number of actions require the wrist today, and it is an essential part of close combat. The work of the wrist, if necessary, must be coordinated with that of the fingers and the forearm, just as we see it in saber fencing These actions, how-

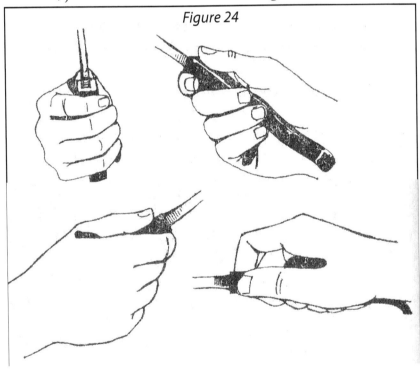

Figure 24

ever, are not for beginners.

The blade can only be directed accurately if it is held correctly. A weak, excessively relaxed grip makes the point insecure. It does not go where the owner wants it to go. The range of motion of a point that hesitates and wobbles around the target will grow larger than desired. The blade will fail in the critical parts of a disengagement. A sluggish hit in the final phase is one among several signs of an improper grip of the blade. Gripping it too hard, however, will tie the weapon to the movement of the arm.

"Canting" the blade (bending the tang slightly inward and downward to a degree that varies with individual preference) must take place when assembling the foil, because it helps:

- The proper handling of the weapon, the natural concurrence of the forearm and the weapon
- Directing the blade toward the opponent's target from the start
- Hitting at an advantageous angle

Use of the parts of the blade

We defend and execute the so-called grazing parries, which take a longer time, *with the guard and the forte (strong part) of the blade.*

We beat and bind (that is attack the blade) and execute the so-called beat parries, contacting at one point, *with the middle of the blade.*

We execute contacts, beats, and changes of binds for the purpose of reconnaissance, preparation *with the foible (weak part) of the blade.*

And finally, we touch *with the point,* provided that the pressure is 500 grams or more.

Work of the fingers

The harmonious work of the fingers ensures:

- The development of gripping without excessive force

- Sensing the blade as a way of developing ability
- Elastically handling the weapon, and
- Ensuring hits on even the smallest surface

Basic Concepts.

The opponents, facing each other, pursue their combat on a conceptual, imaginary line (actually a narrow stripe), which we call the *fencing line* (Fig. 25). In theory, this would connect the heels and the front feet of the two fencers. (During training, the painted sidelines on the floor can be used for practice.) Observing them, if possible, would result in the smallest target surface between the opponents facing each other. During the excitement of actual fencing, this line cannot be maintained consistently. However, the person stepping off the line always has to anticipate the opponent's intention of straightening the line.

Maintaining the fencing line is practical until the distance closes. At close distance, the fencing line cannot be maintained; the arm must be bent if an intended touch is to become a valid hit.

Among beginners, leaving the line can result in a number of mistakes. It can influence weapon handling in an unfortunate direction; it can dissipate the forces required for a fast lunge. Leaving line increases the risk of hitting passé. As the fencer leaves the line, he opens new areas for attack. Leaving the line can make the direct attack on the center of gravity impossible. Finally, by upsetting the fencer's balance, it forces the body and the weapon arm to compensate.

Depending on the distance between the opponents, we can talk about:

- Close distance
- Short distance
- Medium distance
- Long distance

- Out of distance

These distances are theoretical values and they are specified according to the average body size. (The only fixed value is the length of the weapon.) For attacks launched from long and medium distances, the lengths of the steps, and in the case of lunges, the flexibility of the hips, must be taken into account.

- At close distance, footwork plays the main role in creating the opportunity to touch.
- At short distance, a touch can be scored by extending the arm.
- At medium and long distance, footwork becomes necessary.
- It is useless to launch a substantive attack from a position that is out of distance.

The following exercises are useful for showing the three most important distances in a playful way: the coach should be hit from a short distance (if necessary, he should help the student in aiming and directing the blade), and then with short back and forth steps, induce the student to keep the distance while requiring the student to keep the point on the target. (The blade should follow the coach. The point cannot be pushed more than the necessary amount, but it cannot

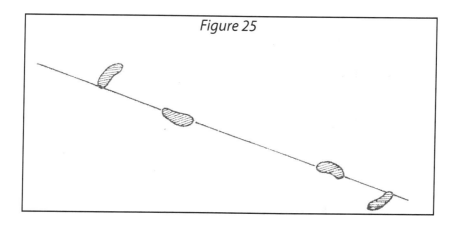

Figure 25

break away from the coach's target surface, not even briefly.) If the coach stops for a longer-shorter period, the student should halt as well. Afterwards, after the coach's verbal command to step back, the student should lunge. With proper assistance, the exercise can also be done with a step and lunge. (With beginners, the individual distances involved will depend on the coach's skills and ability to estimate the distance.) If the coach himself has miscalculated, he should correct the distance between two actions. The recovery from the lunge can be prompted by the coach's advance and/or his verbal command. This exercise can be part of a warm-up for a lesson.

The order of teaching the distances cannot be categorically specified. It can be influenced by the student's skills, the given situation, the coach's mentality, and the chosen method. The coach should establish the distance for beginner students, while for advanced students and competitor fencers, setting the proper distance increasingly becomes the fencer's responsibility.

The standard length of each distance can be changed during teaching when it is necessary. (The difference should be measured in millimeters instead of centimeters.) In the name of correction or in order to spare the student, the coach can stand somewhat closer compared to the usual distance – and slightly further when he wishes to challenge the student.

In the beginning, an unchanging distance is the basis not only for the success of the action, but the development of the student's sense of distance as well. The student learns to perceive changing distance through repeatedly observing of a specific concrete, unambiguous distance.

Numerous types of footwork exercises exist on paper. Nowadays, however, a foil fencer only uses a few of these. Footwork now almost solely comes down to steps and lunges. One of the reasons for this is the continuity of the action (in the past there used to be more standing combat and stalemate), Another reason is the revved-up pace of combat, which makes the use of specific jumps (to take just one example) impossible. In the future, these have to be used only in practice as the tools for developing special skills. Regarding steps and lunges, these have to be taught systematically. Even though there seems to be an increase among those who favor the use of hops (bounces), in place or back and forth, as a new method for preparation and gaining momentum, the domination of the classical back and forth steps is unparalleled in all three weapon types.

Positions of the blades.

The blade positions are typical positions of the weapon arm (Fig. 26). These are:
- The *on guard*
- The *line*
- The *invito*

The *on guard* is a neutral blade position; its criteria are simply set up according to practical aspects. It is an optimal beginning for attacking as well as for defending, which closes to one side, usually towards the sixte, and less frequently towards the octave (as in Fig. 27); that is to say it makes the defense of the closed side unnecessary.

The use of the upper on guard is compulsory by rule at the beginning of the bout and when fencers go back on guard during the bout. (Fencers can change beginning stances and positions immediately after the command to fence.)

The the on guard is in upper or lower line, the elbow of the arm with the weapon should be about the width of the palm or that of the outspread hand in front of the hip. The blade should be positioned slantwise up or down, providing protection for the side of the body that is in line with the weapon arm.

Fencers start from on guard, then begin the combat, and do reconnaissance and preparation. Usually they launch their attacks from this position and this is where they return after unsuccessful attempts.

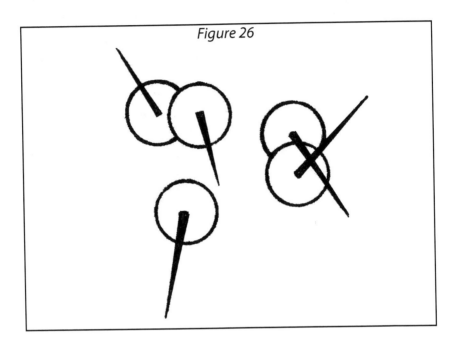

Figure 26

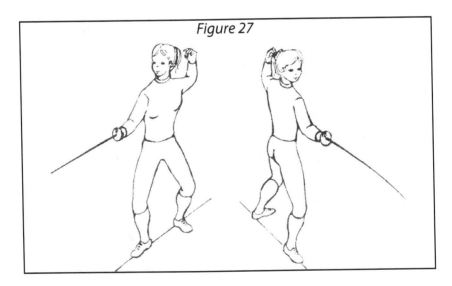

Figure 27

Recently, when there was a multiplication of flicks to the back or shoulders (flicks without disengage in tempo) these fencers chose the saber-like "tierce" as their beginning position in order to proceed with the actions more easily. The change in the signaling machine, luckily, has to some extent put an end to this disgrace to foil fencing.

The *line* is an active, threatening blade position, containing the conventional advantage of the blade (Fig. 28). The requirements regarding it are stated in the rules as well.

Numerous lines exist, since the point – with an extended arm – can be pointing towards any spot on the opponents

Figure 28

target surface. However, we only make a difference between the two typical lines, the so-called upper line (when the point is pointing towards the upper surface of the valid target) and the lower line (when the point is pointing towards the lower surface of the valid target). Their position usually happens in front of the level of the weapon arm's shoulder. During practice, the student must be instructed to use the proper line for the given exercise.

The position of line, like on guard, is not quite an absolutely straight line, due to the angle between the position of the fist and the elbow.

The *invito* (invitation) is a movement compelling an attack; it exposes, uncloaks given parts of the target. The quarte (Fig. 29), septime (Fig. 30), high septime, and septime taken across the target area provide less opportunity for a person preparing to attack.

The sixte (Fig. 31), tierce (Fig 32), octave (Fig. 33), and seconde (Fig. 34), which are in the line of the weapon arm, provide more opportunities.

The invito and the parry are analogous movements. Their

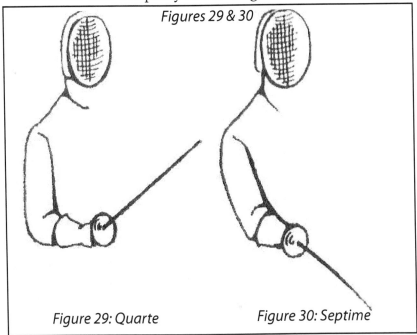

Figures 29 & 30

Figure 29: Quarte   Figure 30: Septime

names indicate their differing purposes: they look the same but have different functions. The invito can be understood as an end position, while the parry will always be a process. The roles become concrete in practice.

It is useless to create a major difference between these two similar movements, which differ only in their aims. The difference is not simply in how large the movement is. In a given situation, the parry can be smaller, while the invito can be larger – but also the other way around.

The blades' relationship to each other is based on the momentary status of the blades held by the two opponents. Taking this into consideration, the following opportunities are given:

1. Both opponents can stand in the same position, that is holding their blades:
    - In a lower- or upper-line on guard
    - In similar or different lines
    - In similar or different lines of invito
2. In case they take up different positions from one another:
    - One fencer can stand in a line, the other one in an invito.
    - One can hold his blade in a line, the other person in "on guard," and finally
    - A fencer can respond with an invito to the other fencer's on guard position.

Not all of the relationships give a free choice in choosing the attack. It is compulsory to start with a beat or press against the lines in order to be eligible to attack.

When fencing, changes in the blade positions are used to fool the opponent, to find out his intentions, in the same way as provocative feints, or advances started with the feet on purpose, the withdrawal of the blades, or the parries imitating reflexes. Therefore, a mobile blade is not only an interlude for one's sake to make the competition more colorful. For beginner children, these exercises can be part of their training to develop their hand and arm muscles.

The *directions* are defined according to a point of reference: the fencing line, the chest, the back, the non-weapon and weapon arm, and the momentary position of the weapon.

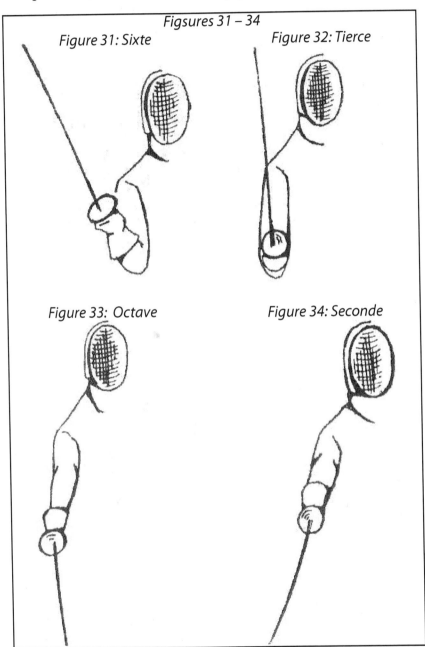

Figsures 31 – 34

Figure 31: Sixte

Figure 32: Tierce

Figure 33: Octave

Figure 34: Seconde

Forward and backward are defined by the fencing line and its direction.

High and low refer to the parts below or above an imaginary horizontal line that can be found in the middle of the target area.

Inside and outside are defined in relation to the non-weapon and weapon hands and arms; that is, inside is the direction moving toward the chest in relation to the weapon arm, while outside is the direction moving towards the back.

From now on, inside-outside will refer to the weapon's position at the moment.

Foil actions and their development. The criteria and technical norms of actions.

Attacks can happen:
- Right after on guard or after proper preparation
- Directly or indirectly
- Targeting the open or opening line
- Without any obstacles by a direct thrust
- Deflecting the opposing blade
- Changing the line of attack by passing around the guard or the tip
- Targeting the lower or upper target area.

We differentiate between simple and compound attacks. Simple attacks consist of one movement, while a compound attack consists of two or more movements.

Among the simple attacks, direct thrusts require the least amount of time and travel the shortest distance, disengagements require more time, while flicks require the most amount of time and travel the longest distances.

The direct thrust only requires the extension of the arm when the distance is short. The point must advance from on guard straightforward upwards along the hypotenuse of an imaginary right triangle (this can only be done, by leading with the point from the beginning). It should hit the targeted spot at the last moment.

Most direct thrusts end in the high line (Fig. 35). They are rarely directed deliberately towards the lower sector. The coach should provide help during the first attempts if necessary: he should hold the point with his unarmed hand, while he guides the student's guard with his weapon, keeping it in the right direction. He should repeat this a few times while adding verbal instructions, and afterwards leave it to the student to do future attacks on his own. When encountering mistakes, the coach can correct them in a similar way.

Figure 35

Practical experience shows – though this may seem somewhat illogical – that it is better to begin teaching the direct thrust from medium distance (Fig. 36). At short distance, a number of beginners feel that there is not enough space to do the exercise. As a result they either do not extend their arms together with their weapons or they unnecessarily add their shoulder into the thrust, ruining the end position. It is easier to avoid all of these mistakes when doing it from a medium distance.

The fencer first encounters the conformity of the hand and the feet, dictated by the rules and logic, during the learning of the direct thrusts from a medium distance. The hand and the arm must already be in motion when the front foot leaves the ground. A direct attack beginning with the foot is only

Figure 36

effective to fool frightened people. (Though sometimes it can result in touches, this is not a reason for this to be taught). However, it is a principle (though one can revert from this for tactical reasons) that the lunge must be launched prior to the complete extension of the arm. The arm's extension must be timed according to the second half of the step during a step forward – lunge. Starting with the foot, either earlier or later, is a technical mistake. This can also be remedied throughout the process of training.

Less coordinated students – in order to experience the

length of the arm extension – should do partial, quarter, half, and three-quarters long arm stretches, a number of times before doing the lunge.

The direct thrust should be done according to one's own tempo first and then according to the coach's signal, that is according to a tempo from the arm or the feet. This educational order can be followed for all of the actions that naturally allow it. (Disengage in tempo thrusts can only be taught with a tempo from the hand from the beginning.)

It is only possible in theory to have successful touches with the use of direct thrusts from long distance, even when the tempo is enormous or there is a huge difference between the skills of the fencers. That is why this should only be part of the training program as an exercise aiming to develop skills.

Theory calls the thrusts disengaging around the guard "change thrusts" or "disengage thrusts," while those disengaging around the tip as flicks (coupés) or disengage flicks (coupés). (These are twin action pairs, which is why their techniques are the same, but their time of use is different.)

Progressiveness – the continual forward motion of the point – can be achieved from the beginning in case of change and disengage thrusts. In the case of flicks and coupés and disengage flicks and coupés, this can only happen in the second half of the action.

The execution of the spiral, screw-like, advancing movement of the change and disengage in tempo thrusts depends on the distance. At a shorter distance, the extension should begin during the disengagement; at medium distance, the disengagement should take place during the extension. The amplitude is determined by the size of the obstacle in the way. The guard can be disengaged in a well-rounded, bigger way, while the blade can be disengaged with a smaller, flatter movement. In an optimal case, the disengaging blade runs parallel to the opposing blade, which is in the way almost until the finish.

The change and disengage in tempo thrusts can end in the same line as the beginning (Fig. 37) or the opposite line (Fig. 38). In the first case, the blade, due to the work of the fingers, runs along the upper and lower lines of an imaginary circle, and in the second case, it draws the same circle's left and right side in the air.

The critical part of the disengagement in the upper line is the second half, while for the lower line, it is the first half. Beginners usually get tangled up with the coaches' hands or guards in these phases. Gravity can help in the beginning of the upper line disengagements and the end of the lower line disengagements.

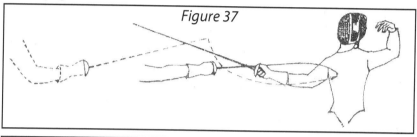

Figure 37

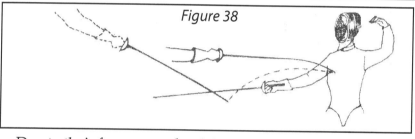

Figure 38

Due to their frequency also, it is practical to teach disengagements around the guard by teaching the disengage in tempo thrust. The students should stand in a line (this way we can get rid of the useless involvement of the hand and the arms) and they should disengage multiple times from the slow and continuous quartes and sixtes of the coach. This should be followed by the disengagement of the advancing and retreating quartes and sixtes. One should only allow the use of a lunge after a correct series. This is followed by the combination of lunges with the exercise. The coach should not only use simple binds, he should incorporate semi-circle or circle binds as well to assist the thrusts. In the end the students should practice disengage beats. Due to the blade's faster motion, faster disengagements will be required.

The flicks (Fig. 39), like the disengagements around the guard, can be done during a tempo and after engagements with the opponent's blade. Coupés are in the upper line almost without exception. The prerequisite for their execution is the steeper position of the opponent's blade or the intention to engage the blade in such a way.

The work of the fingers and the wrists are enough for flicks at medium distance. As the distance narrows, the success of the coupés becomes more dependent on the elbows.

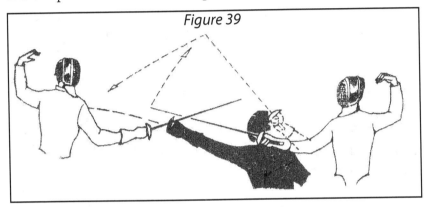

Figure 39

Thrusts can be done:

- Moving the hand, the arm, the blade in a straight line (Fig. 40)
- While in motion, pushing the fist towards the direction of the opponent's blade (Fig. 41)
- Maintaining contact with the opponent's blade from the beginning to the end of the thrust (Fig. 42)
- Moving the hand and blade away from the opponent's blade while thrusting. (Fig. 43)

These thrusts are not equally common. Foil actions usually end in a straight line.

It is useful to move with the fist in the direction of the opponent's blade during counter thrusts only in the last cadence. Here, larger movements towards the inside and smaller movements towards the outside will be needed to have the proper opposition.

Figures 40 – 43: Thrusts

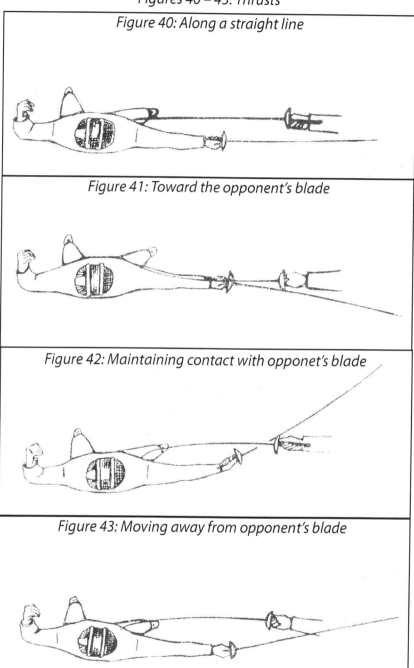

Figure 40: Along a straight line

Figure 41: Toward the opponent's blade

Figure 42: Maintaining contact with opponet's blade

Figure 43: Moving away from opponent's blade

In the case of bind thrusts, where the opponents' blades are held in a firm line producing opposition, the guard – in front of the opponent's blade – advances parallel to the point on its separate way. Logically, the size of the opposition is larger when it comes to inside bind thrusts. Foil fencers use this thrust type only as ripostes nowadays.

The finishing positions of the opposition thrusts and bind thrusts are often strangely similar, even though the blades meeting points greatly differ from each other. During an opposition thrust, the fist is pushed to the side, and there is contact between the two blades in the last third of the movement. In case of a bind thrust, there is contact between the blades throughout the whole action. This is instantaneous with bind thrusts and flanconades, while it is late with disengage in tempo thrusts and usually it happens during the motion towards the second half and the end of the movement.

The creation of angles is a product of close combat resulting in the closing the distance. This is the only way to get in front of, under, or above the target area in a closed distance.

Lines can and must be diverted from their positions with beats and binds. The criteria detailed in the rules are judged by the jury during competitions. There are no rules regarding the beats and binds used to figure out the intentions of one's partner. They can even be symbolic.

It is more practical to use a beat against those who hold their blade in line loosely, while it is more practical to use a bind against those who hold a firm line. (This is far from being a compulsory rule.) One can find out information about the types of lines during reconnaissance.

A dry, clicking sound signals the meeting of the beat with the opponent's blade at a single point. A specific sound resulting from the friction of the blades signals the binds, which take a longer time.

A *bind* is a blade movement following engagement, which the attacker uses, usually with the middle of his blade, to deflect the opponent's blade from a threatening position by a pushing move in relation to the distance that exists at the moment.

A *beat* is an energetic movement that happens for a short time. It is most effective when we use our fingers to direct the middle of our blade against the weak pat of the opponent's blade. The blade doing the beat must stop its motion where the attacked blade was, in order to limit the action. The main role for this relies on the fingers.)

Besides against lines, one can use a beat against blades in the on guard position, or positions showing a slight tendency for an invitation, in order to fill the distance, to estimate the strength of the grip, to relax the grip, to offset the blade due to reflexes, or to increase the target sector. (It is useless to do proper beats and binds against full invitos.)

The *grazing beat (sforzo)* is a hybrid action, the mixture of a beat and a bind. Its use is recommended for coupés in the upper line. The movement is beating and transporting the attacked blade at the same time. It is good for weakening the grip and for a figurative "disarmament" of the opponent.

The names of the beats and binds are the same as the names of the invitos, like the size of their moves. Thus there are quarte, sixte, seconde (octave), and septime beats and binds. (A pronated seconde beat or bind is more effective than a supinated octave beat or bind because of the turning of the hand.)

The beats and binds can be:
- Simple
- Semi-circular
- Circular
- And (according to some schools) change beats or binds as well. (A change is done with a circle-like movement *after one's own or the opponent's engagement.*)

The beats and binds can partner with each other during bouts. The first member of a compound action is usually a bind. A beat rarely overtakes an immediate chance for a bind.

The dynamic equivalent in footwork of the bind-thrust attacks from long distances is the step-and-lunge, for beats it is the balestra. (Although the use of this latter has become rare nowadays, the balestra remains an important part of the training program for the development of skills.) The beats and binds can be followed by simple or complex actions.

For touches through a short distance:

- One can use direct thrusts or
- Disengage around the guard.

The coupés following beats, binds require longer distances even if the circumstances are most favorable.

Bind thrust attacks can only be executed following the binds. This thrust type does not release the opponent's blade and the fencer's blade slides forward along the opponent's it until it hits. The inner bind thrusts (*filos*), require vigorous contribution from the fist. If this thrust type finishes on the opponent's side, below the arm, it is called a flanconade. This follows the quarte for fencers with the same hands, or sixte for fencers with opposite hands.

The easiest way to teach beats and binds to beginners is to teach them in the form of beats and counter-beats, binds, and counter-binds. The beginning beat or bind gives the student the sample movement he has to follow and copy. The response beats and binds are to be done like the coach's, without any delay, with the same force, amplitude, and speed. The sound of the blades meeting also helps the student. The student may may be asked to respond with the same number of beats-binds as the coach performed, or with a different number. The student may respond to the coach's beat with one or two, the coach's double beat with double or simple beats. If the coach pauses with the sequence of beats-binds, the student should pause as well. The student should only initiate when the coach tells him to. However, it should not always be the coach who decides who attacks or many responses the partner gives. Half the tme it should be the student's job.

Attacks can be defended with:
- Distance
- Parries
- Correctly timed and executed counterattacks

Distance does not solve anything on its own; it might only postpone the defeat. The parry will only be successful if partnered with a riposte.

Italo Santelli thought, "The counterattack is a gamble, but the parry can be developed with hard work." If the defender misses the tempo or is not able to measure the correct path of the blade, he will be touched.

The parry and the counterattack are partnered with footwork in practice. This increases the efficiency of the defense.

Parries can be executed:
- Standing, in line, in an invitation, or from engagement
- In the same line as in the beginning or changing the line

They can be taken
- Horizontally: in the high or low line (Fig. 44)
- Vertically: the parries on the same side, but in the opposite line (Fig. 45)
- Diagonally: the parries on the opposite side and in the opposite line (Fig 46)

Their movement can be:
- Simple resistant
- Semi-circular
- Circular

The semi-circular and circular parries are performed with some characteristics of a beat or bind. (These parries are the most important, most frequently used, and the ones efficient for almost every action.)
- During feint attacks they follow or wait for the opponent's blade; that is, they are timed for the last part of the opponent's movement. (During defense against feints, only the last parry has to be a proper, full parry.)

Figures 44 – 47: Types of Parries

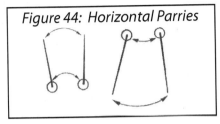

Figure 44: Horizontal Parries

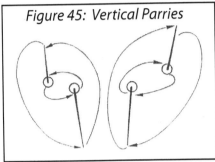

Figure 45: Vertical Parries

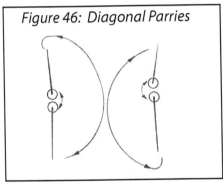

Figure 46: Diagonal Parries

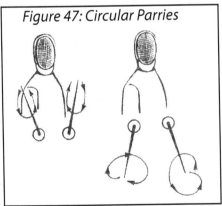

Figure 47: Circular Parries

With the help of an imaginary square or rectangle in front of the fencer, one can demonstrate the position of each parry compared to the student's target surface, the position of the parries or their path in the air, and the transitions that can be created among them. If the fencer is right-handed, the quarte will be in the parallelogram's upper left corner, the sixte in the upper right corner, the seconde and octave in the lower right corner, and the septime in the lower left corner. If the fencer starts off the parries with a quarte and follows the four sides of the square (rectangle) back and forth, the simple parries will be done. It is easy to parry and go from quarte to sixte, from sixte to seconde, from seconde to septime, and from septime to quarte and backward on this same path from quarte to septime, from septime to seconde, from seconde to sixte, and finally from sixte to quarte.

The four semicircular parries follow the diagonals. A semicircle is from quarte to seconde, from seconde to quarte and from sixte to septime, and from septime to sixte.

The circular movements launched outside from the four corners will come back to where they started from, drawing the four circular parries in the air (Fig. 47).

- If the fencer is in quarte position, he can take simple sixte, simple septime, semicircle seconde, and circle quarte.
- Starting from sixte, a simple quarte, simple seconde, semicircle septime, and circle sixte.
- Starting from seconde, a simple septime, simple sixte, semicircle quarte, and circle seconde.
- Starting from septime, simple seconde, simple quarte, semicircle sixte, and circle septime.

The simple (resistant) parries require the shortest distance.

The real territory for the beat parries is in the first line. Some *pico* parries in the right moment can have "preventive," delaying traits. The parries containing friction taken closer to the body need more time to launch the riposte. This especially applies to parries used in close combat and the ripostes from them.

Parries can be made with hands in a supinated or pronated position. The size of the supination or pronation varies; usually it is the largest in case of seconde and prime. Prime – the pronated cousin of septime – is the same as in saber, with the same movement and same end position. If necessary, these parries can end up next to or behind the target surface, thanks to the turn. In intense combats, the pronated parries, which are able to close off the plane, serve the fencer better than the supinated parries, which tend to defend only the lines.

The arcs of the pronated parries are smoother due to the rotation of the forearm compared to the unchanging position of the supinated hand. Circle parries move in a misshapen ellipse, rather than in actual circles.

The supinated parries can be changed into pronated parries while in motion. This is how an octave becomes a circle seconde for example, or a sixte a circle tierce.

Parries should be taken as far forward as possible. A parry taken farther forward operates near the apex of an imaginary horizontal cone, while a parry taken farther back is working at the base of that cone. Therefore, the closer a parry gets to the target, whether out of necessity or by mistake, the bigger it must become in order to intercept the attacking blade.

A fencer who parries while retreating will sooner or later have no alternative but to change the line in which the parry is taken. That is how the quarte and the tierce will end up on the lower line and the seconde and prime in the upper line.

The raised or dropped parries narrow the group of applied actions for the defender. Bind ripostes, implemented in a strong angled version, become dominating in close combat.

In addition to simple, semicircle, and circle parries, the so-called ceding parries also exist. These can only be used to defend against filos and flanconades. Of these, ceding parries against the bind sixte thrust and the high septime are the ones that are most comfortable. The ceding parry begins with a blade movement in the direction that the opponent is trying to take one's blade (ceding). The movement done by the point and the fist start off in opposite directions. While the blades are in contact, the fencer's blade then makes a cone-like movement where the end position is the top of the two blades' meeting point. The movement is much easier to demonstrate or to perform than to describe.

The crossed high sixte or high septime type (Fig. 48) or the effective saber-like quintes are the most effective parries to guard against coupés and flicks in the upper line. The riposte launched from the latter is similar to the side cut used in saber.

Average parries can be positioned in space by:

- The distance of the arm, elbow from the target surface
- The direction of the blade
- The point's digression to the side from one of our body parts

In *quarte*, the arm is bent at the elbow about a hand's-breadth in front of the navel. The blade faces diagonally forward, upwards, and inwards. The point is inside, at eye height, a *maximum* of one palm beyond the limit of the body. Quarte may be taken in either a (semi-) pronated or supinated position (Fig. 49).

In *sixte*, the elbow is in front of and in the line of the hip. The blade is an unbent continuation of the forearm and it faces diagonally forward and upwards. The fist and guard are shoulder high, the point is at eye level on the weapon arm side somewhat outside the line of the eye (Fig. 50).

In *tierce* (the pronated version of sixte) the arm is more bent due to the rotation of the forearm, making the parry deeper and closer to the fencer's own target compared to the sixte. The blade faces forward and upwards at a steeper diagonal (Fig. 51).

In *seconde*, the fist sinks under the shoulder about the distance of a palm. The elbow, as in the sixte, is facing outwards with a slight bend. The point is maximum a span from the line of the hip. The blade and the arm form a small slope (Fig. 52).

Figure 48: High sixte – septime parry

Figure 49: Quarte parry

Figure 50: Sixte parry

Figure 51: Tierce parry

Figure 52: Seconde parry

Figure 53: Octave parry

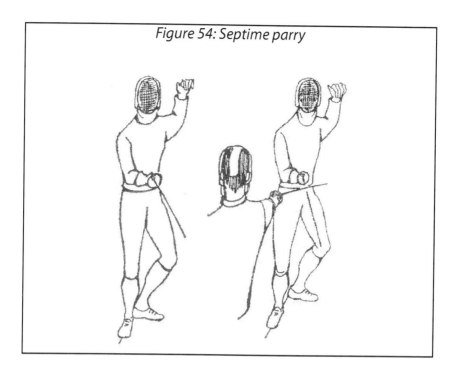

Figure 54: Septime parry

Figure 55: Prime parry

In the *octave,* the seconde's supinated equivalent, the arm is slightly bent. The elbow is almost 9 inches in front of the hip and in line with it. The fist is outside, while the point is facing towards the inside a little. The blade makes a slight slope downwards, towards the inside (Fig. 53).

In the *septime,* the fist is in the line and about the height of the shoulder of the non-weapon arm. The blade tends to be directed a bit downward and outside from this line (Fig. 54).

In a *prime* parry (this is the septime's pronated equivalent) the forearm, bent at the elbow, crosses the target almost horizontally. The fist is situated at the height of the shoulder of the non-weapon arm and in line with it. The blade is steeper than a septime parry, looking downwards and outwards diagonally (Fig. 55).

The fastest way to teach and correct the simple, semicircle, and circle parries, is with the help of the transfers. This involves the fewest mistakes almost from the beginning,

During a lesson, the coach should place his weapon on the side of the student's guard where he wants the parry to be done. He should keep the contact and allow the student to move his blade to the other side for a simple parry. to the other line on the opposite side, for a semicircle parry, and with a "circular" (elliptical) movement back to the starting-position for a circle parry, .

As long as the coach does not resist and the student is running the point along the proper arc, the two blades will stay in contact with each other the whole time. This way, the coach can help and at the same time control the path of the blade, the offset with the point, the competent range and the limitation at the proper spot. In order to learn and become accustomed to these important technical elements, the students can assist each other similarly after lessons.

Ripostes take place after parries:

- In the same line as the attackers blade or switching lines
- Away from the opponent's blade or with bind, using its resistance, and in close combat, even

with transfer (the antecedent of filos and flanks can only be grazing parries)
- Disengaging with one movement in the direction of the guard or the point
- With a feint

Depending on the distance, the riposte can be made:
- In close combat, with a bent arm
- With extension of the arm
- With a lunge
- With a fleche

Theoretically the possibilities for a counter-riposte are the same as for a riposte. But as soon as it is time for pro and contra manifestations, the fencer relies on his instinct, trying to solve the exercises in the easiest way with the least risks. (This might be the reason why solutions containing feints are so rare.)

Riposte series can be used to train the competitors' hands and arms in a special way and to intensify the joint movement of parry-ripostes. Two (maximum three) parry ripostes must be connected as a whole, without any delays, and accelerating, for the riposte series to be successful. (Series with more parts show a slowing tendency at the end.) If necessary, to avoid the muscles becoming stiff, shorter-longer pauses have to be implemented between series. With the introduction of transfers, the exercises can be expanded. The lesson's main part must contain ripostes.

As soon as the fencer can do his exercise at an adequate level and speed, the coach should sometimes parry the first, second, or third riposte, making the student do a counter-riposte.

It is important to keep in mind the principle of gradation, taking into consideration that during this form of exercise, one has to conjure highly complex things to life, based on rhythm, speed, and form. The possibilities should be expanded based on the fencer's skills and development. The first series should build on the easiest, most obvious actions.

The *feint attack, feint riposte* can be:

155

- Single, double, multiple
- Simple, circular (the feint becomes circular due to the reacting circle-parry) or
- Mixed (mixed feints only happen from double feints and above)

The intermediate or last stages of the feints, regardless of their number or type, are always disengage in tempo thrusts or disengage in tempo flicks.

Feints can be introduced with:

- A direct thrust
- A change thrust
- A disengage in tempo thrust
- A coupé
- A coupé in tempo
- Varieties of these combined with beats and binds (with the exception of the disengage in tempo thrust and the coupé in tempo)

The purpose of the feints is to fool the opponent, and if launched from afar, to fill the distance. Generally, their timing depends on the partner's behavior (Are we talking about a calm or frightened, nervous fencer?). The typical timing of simple feints can be short-long, long-short, short-short, or long-long. Logically, the number of variants regarding double feints is greater.

In case of a short feint, the shortness of distance has to be compensated with dynamics. That is, the feint has to be launched with a push-like movement. In case of a long feint with a short finish, the feint must also overlap somewhat with the lunge for the movement to evoke the desired effect against a calm fencer.

The feint is successful if:

- It imitates the appearance of a real thrust; that is to say, it is suggestive
- Its blade is continuously advancing; that is to say, it is progressive.

Feints can be parried with the number of the feints plus one movement. The last, complete parry can be simple, semicircle, or circle. The mediate, so-called reacting parries can be executed with only half, one-third of their normal amplitude if the feints are recognized in time.

Feints can be neutralized with *following* parries or if changing the line, then with *anticipating or intercepting* parries. For example, a simple single feint in the upper line can be parried with a quarte – sixte, as a following parry, or by quarte – septime, as an anticipating or intercepting parry, where the attacking blade is already stopped in the middle of the process.

Reacting parries can be omitted if the distances make it possible and the feints are recognized in time. The defender only concentrates on one parry, attempting to parry the last segment of the feint attack. This creates the illusion for outsiders that the attacker has fallen on the defender's blade trying to parry, while the defender has fallen asleep while trying to attack.

Feints are not only useful for attacks; they are useful for ripostes as well. In such instances, the numbers of feints, due to the short distance, are limited. Most feint ripostes are simple single feints.

When learning the feints, the beginner first must get accustomed to the blade's continuous advancing movement at medium distance, instead of learning any particular feint. The coach should assist this with a quarte or sixte contact. From this position, the student should advance the blade with four or five progressive disengages until the arm is fully extended, and then the same number of progressive retractions back to the start position. The coach's weapon should remain motionless throughout the whole exercise. This should be practiced on the spot in the beginning and then with continuous back and forth steps, and only after practicing this exercise is it allowed and required for the last disengage to end in a hit.

The attack can be *renewed* if the defender:

- Parries, but still owes a riposte (he riposted slowly or not at all)

- Parries, but retreats instead of riposting, or
- With or without a parry, removes himself from the coverage of the attack

The starting position of the renewed attacks is the lunge or the arm's already extended position.

The following footwork can be used for a renewed attack:

- If the defender parried and stayed on the spot, it is enough to stretch the lunge somewhat, by placing the front foot forward (this is short distance for the renewed thrust)
- If the opponent misses the riposte and retreats, recovering forward to on guard with the rear foot, then lunging again or a doing a fleche (this is medium distance for the renewed thrust)
- And finally, the fleeing opponent can only be reached with a complex footwork from a lunge, for example the radoppio – step forward – lunge or the radoppio step forward – fleche. (This is long distance for the renewed attack.)

The risk of the renewed attack grows in proportion to the distance.

Renewed attacks can be executed with:

- Angular thrusts
- Change thrusts, as long as the distance has grown and the opponent opened a line
- Beat – direct or beat – change thrusts
- Of the feint attacks, only the straight thrust or beat thrust – simple single feint can be used.

When practicing renewed attacks during lessons, the coach should imitate the defender or in the case of missed counter-ripostes he should imitate the role of the attacker.

Close combat and its peculiarities.

Combat at close distance can be intentional or unintentional. It can happen as a result of both of the parties' initiation, simply as a result of the applied footwork, or as a esult of the weapon actions accompanying the footwork.

All of the points of the valid target that are usually un-reachable from middle or long distances because they are covered, or are in a disadvantageous position or angle, can be threatened during close combat.

Competitors tend to leave the fencing line and face each other or fight side by side. This usually causes a change in the angle of the thigh within the fencing position.

The situation requires technical solutions that are unique to the distance. For example, the weapon arm can only func-tion with a bent elbow.

In close combat, the image of the parry usually changes when the fencer closes the distance, striving not only to close the line, but the plane as well. This is how, for instance the quarte ends up deep in the lower line with a steep blade (Fig. 56) (the fencer often helps this by descending into a deep crouch) or the seconde, tied together with the stretching of the knees, raising it high above the fencer's shoulder, into the highest line.

Twisting, ducking, and leaning come to the front, instead of the uses of parries with the blade. Since there is no space for parries, these are often the only means a fencer can avoid a touch.

Continued attacks performed at an angle dominate at close distance. One of the characteristics of this is the "fork-like" thrust, which horizontally disengages the blade itself by pulling the elbow back.

Figure 56: Low quarte in close combat

Close combat is a borderline case; often only a little separates it from corps à corps. In such instances, the jury's job is more difficult as well. Often the one who steps out of close distances wins the touch. That is why close combat must be fought until the referee calls "halt.".

Progression of the actions and the tactical ladder.

The linear progression of the actions starts with the attack, followed by the defender's response, his parry-riposte action, and closes with the attacker's counter-response (that is, with his counter-riposte). Nowadays, longer phrases than these are not as common anymore.

The tactical ladder begins with the counterattack; this is met with second intention. This can be answered in turn with a feint counter-attack. The sequence is finally closed with the finta in tempo, the counter thrust given during the feint counter-attack.

The linear progression is more common in foil than in the combat-type epee.

The counter-attack is an active defending mode, a contracted form of attacking and defending that substitutes for the parry-riposte. The aim of the thrusting parry or parrying thrust can be neutralizing the opponent's action right from the beginning, or intercepting the blade that is already on its way.

A counter-attack can succeed if:

- The opponent lacks the logical hand-foot coordination, namely he starts with his feet
- While in motion, he retracts his arm, thus losing the right of way (priority)
- He tries to bind or beat the blade, but does so with large movements
- He experiments with attacks or ripostes made up of multiple feints.

The assurances of success:

- A split second start

- Energetic execution
- Charting the path of the attacking blade

One can give a touch as a counter-attack with:

- *Direct thrust* against every action launched with the feet (foot tempo), every coupé (flick), and most feint attacks during their intermediate cadence
- *Disengage in tempo thrust* against those experimenting with binds and beats
- *Opposition counterattack thrusts* for the ending movement of most simple actions, most feint attacks, and feint ripostes

In order to achieve the correct relative speed, it is useful to do most counter-attacks with a smaller-larger lunge (the actual length varies).

The person doing the counter-attack sometimes tries to turn or duck to make the opponent's blade miss or hit passé, though the counter-attacker's movements never depart from the methods and sizes stated in the rulebook.

Occasionally, competitors with long arms, having a significant superiority in height, attempt to apply the epee-like counterattack thrust. Since the success of this in foil is really questionable, it would be a bold thing to add this solution into the repertoire and teach it systematically.

The disengage in tempo thrust is a classic action of foil fencing and one of the most frequently used counter-attacking methods. (In epee, this title goes to the change counterattack thrust.)

Disengage in tempo thrusts can be applied against most types of binds and beats (simple, semicircle, circle, change) as long as there is some mistake in their execution and it is noticed in time. Binds and beats that start with the point and tend to accelerate along a short path cannot be avoided. Only beats and binds that start relatively slowly or approach rather noticeably can be stopped with a disengage in tempo thrust.

Counter-thrusts during feint attacks can be applied in the first cadence, when the feint is launched, instead of an effective parry; in the second cadence, during the parry taken for the feint's first movement; and in the last cadence, reacting to most of the intermediate movements.

It is enough to cross the path of the line (usually the attacker's blade gets stuck on this). In the last cadence, opposition becomes a necessity in order to successfully divert the blade.

The counterattack thrusts have to be executed high, in place of the simple quarte or seconde parries, or low, in place of the simple sixte, or septime.

If the counterattack thrust is substituting for a circle quarte or circle seconde, the partner must be targeted in the upper line, instead of the lower circle sixte and circle septime.

The second intention's broader scope contains all of those tactical manifestations when the competitor does not always intend to give a touch with his first action.

The classical second intention in foil mainly deals with disengage in tempo thrust counterattacks. Against these, the parry is generally no more than a simple parry following the shortest path. (Competitors apply fewer second intentions against opposition thrusts in live bouts.) The most typical of these have to be practiced during lessons. The method of execution from long distance is as follows: the chosen solution to trigger the disengage in tempo or counterattack thrust has to be launched and finished at the same time as the first half of the advance. The parry should happen when the step is closed, while the riposte after that, with the required footwork based on the distance or a simple arm extension.

Parry-ripostes against counterattacks (perceived or induced) have a narrower scope. They comprise the second step of second intention actions with more extensive progressions.

The feint counterattack (finta in tempo) is a classical counteraction of the second intention. The counterattack is made up of the feint and the disengage from the parry taken against the feint (theoretically this parry can be simple, semicircle, or circle). We use this against opponents who are preparing for a second intention from the beginning. The simple single feints from disengage in tempo thrusts turn out to be the most successful.

The counterattack thrust, (the counter-tempo), used against the feint counterattack (finta in tempo) completes the tactical progression of the foil actions.

The attacker starts first and executes the counter-riposte also during the technical buildup of the actions. (The defender's job in the second step is the parry-riposte.)

In case of a further progression, the roles are as follows: the defender makes the counter-attack, the attacker performs the second intention, and the defender, in turn, performs the counter-tempo.

During the lesson, the coach must play the role

- Of the attacker when the student counterattacks
- Of the counterattacked in case of a second intention
- Of the person wanting to do a second intention in case of a feint counterattack
- And finally, the role of the person trying a finta in tempo in case of a counter-tempo.

VI. Tactics: Theory and Practice

Tactics consists of the logical use of the tools at hand during a bout. It is a measure of the fencer's nervous system, temperament, and practical intelligence.

The qualities that play a role in the clashes between the thoughts of the opponents can be developed with the use of bout-like lessons and paired exercises designed for this purpose.

No matter how broad a fencer's foundations may be, his technical repertoire will shrink with time around a so-called family of actions, which will have members from the line of actions promising the highest success. A competitor will most likely, if not always, try to reach his aims and implement his ideas with the use of such actions in critical moments. The range of actions cannot be too narrow; it has to be bordered with solutions that can replace the actions that are momentarily ineffective, even if the roles will not be exactly the same and will work only for a shorter-longer period of time.

Tactical possibilities are proportionate to technical development. The more actions, variants, and combinations a person knows, the more tactical possibilities he will have – in theory. The question is how much of this a fencer, a competitor, can realize during a bout.

One can only deal with tactics if the fencer has a solid knowledge of technique. If the fencer has to pay attention to technical execution, even for mere moments during a bout, his ideas will be at risk. The best tactics can be doomed to failure because of technical mistakes arising from excitement. The tools of attacking and parrying relate to each other proportionally. The opponent can exploit the situation if a major difference happens at the expense of either one.

The alleged or actual advantage of the left-handed fencers can be traced back to two things.

The first is that since there are many more right-handed fencers than left-handed (although the latter's numbers are increasing somewhat), right-handed fencers encounter left-handers less often. There are fewer occasions for getting used to the opposite handedness and getting over the hindrances connected to them.

The second can be found in the simple fact that right-handed fencers encounter the stronger quarte, which is more difficult to disengage from, instead of the sixte they are already to on their inner side among same-handed fencers. Inexperienced fencers often become entangled while disengaging from the quarte. The disadvantage felt against left-handed fencers can be decreased by practicing bouts with left-handed fencers and receiving left-handed lessons.

The student can gain tactical knowledge through:
- Knowledge presented by the coach
- Personal experience
- Purposeful observation of the opponents, striving for consequences, regarding the reasons of both success and of failure. The gained experiences must be stored for their fruitful use in the future.

In order to win:
- The opponent's will has to be broken
- One must take control into one's own hand, but not necessarily only through attacking
- The opponent has to be misled
- By countering his intentions, we have to limit our opponent's ability to use his strengths.
- We must maintain our cool, self-confidence, ability to make sudden, unexpected, decisions and to act on them, so our best ideas prevail.

It is unnecessary to waste tactics on opponents who are undeveloped when it comes to technique. Such opponents have to be beaten with proper technique alone.

However, opponents who have an advantage in technique have to be defeated with the help of tactics, avoiding complicated solutions.

- Fencers who are good at attacking have to be pushed to defend; those who are good in defending have to be pushed to attack.
- Against fencers who are good in counterattacks, one should apply second intention; those who excel in second intention should be defeated with finta in tempo.
- Momentum can be created against those who like blade attacks by withdrawing the blade.
- One should avoid the distance favored by the opponent.
- Opponents operating with feint attacks and feint ripostes can be intercepted with counterattacks.
- If the opponent relies on a series of linked actions, he can be frustrated by added pauses.
- Differences in height can be neutralized by the correction of the distance.

It is easier to shift between possibilities when a fencer's attacking and defending abilities are roughly equal. Using the patterns constructively also depends on the routine of the competitor.

A fencer can be active or passive.

The active:

- Tries to control his partner
- Creates his own plans
- Monitors the bout continuously
- Accelerates the fights
- Often attacks
- Leaves little time for the interlude

The passive:

- Surrenders the initiative
- Often waits
- Mostly eacts to his opponent

- Parries more often than attacking.

With time, fencers will be either attacking or defending in style as competitors. There are fewer of the latter.

Every bout is characterized by the duality of premeditation and improvisation. It is not certain that both of these abilities will be found in every fencer. The timing of the switch from one to the other is crucial. The previously roughed-out tactics have to be modified during the bout if necessary.

During bouts where the results have no importance, meaning that is there is nothing for the fencer to lose, there seems to be a limitless possibility to study the opponent, to experiment, to balance the circumstances, and to switch the actions.

When facing stronger opponents, psychological factors can help balance out technical-tactical disadvantages.

The psychological effect of the first touch can be greater for a passive fencer than an active one.

In case of need, one has to refrain from continued use even of successful actions. Not everyone can stop in time!

Even weaker opponents have to be taken seriously. If a fencer forgets this, he can encounter unpleasant surprises; a careless bout can end in a loss.

The preparation, this part of the bout that can be theoretically separated, is nothing more than the play of the blade and the distance, colored with changing pace, intensity, and breaks. Its task is to *find out*:

- How does the opponent react to expected and unexpected attacks?
- What are the tangible signs of his attention and inattention?
- What attacks is he planning to use and how does he want to execute them.

The opponent's intentions for parrying (depending on the opponent) can be mapped by false attacks that are executed up to half or two-thirds of the way.

The opponent's alertness can be decreased by calm movements of the weapons and with a sedative type of footwork.

One can draw attacks by offering the opponent the most advantageous positions and distance.

One's own intention has to be camouflaged with apparently careless movements.

One must produce believable actions to fool the opponent.

A fencer must think through the tasks connected to attacking and defending in a rather short time compared to the length of the bout. This cannot be done without the separation of the attention with specific aims in mind. The fact that a fencer must pay attention to two things, which can change to their opposite at the last moment, requires fast information processing. The fencer in this is helped by

- Understanding the situation as it develops
- Penetrating the opponent's thought processes
- The ability to improvise

More attention, more time, and more actions have to be spent on unknown opponents. Sometimes, fragments of this process are enough against familiar opponents. The instinctive moves have to be made intentional and adjusted to the individual's skills during training.

Effective attacking and defending actions follow reconnaissance and preparation. Competitors prefer *attacking* out of these actions, since they direct the background for these. One cannot attack without breaks because of the time used for preparation.

Attacks can be made up of premeditated moves or ones formed during the fight. Temperament and activity is necessary for their execution. These can arise from the fencer's

- Personality
- Psychological superiority
- Awareness of technical or tactical development.

The parry is the main tool of defense. The reason for this:

- Its risk is less compared to counterattacks
- Even a blade that eluded us in the beginning can be caught up with a timely parry
- Each parry offers a number of possible riposte

- The counterattack, conversely:
- Is one-off and unrepeatable
- There is no time or space to continue the counterattack or to correct faulty moves.

Those who use the parries safely do not react to feints, or only with half parries. They wait with their actual parries for the last possible moment, when the defending blade cannot be disengaged. The ripostes from such parries can have a demoralizing effect.

The fencer who has been pushed to the rear borderline can only advance through aggression, a tough counterattack.

However, it is dangerous to thoughtlessly storm those fencers who have strong defensive abilities and feel comfortable standing on the rear borderline or close to it.

Parries cannot be planned ahead in case of surprise attacks. The fencer improvises in such cases.

The prerequisite of the premeditated parries are intentional control over the opponent's moves or recognizing them in time.

Parries can be substituted by counterattacks. This is what active defense means.

Those executed in the first cadence have better chances than the ones initiated in the second and third steps.

The disengage in tempo thrusts have the best chances. It is enough to seize the perfect moment for these. For counterattack thrusts, the line of the attack must be measured by centimeters for a successful opposition.

Passive defense can mean the disruption of the distance, a parry without a riposte, or evasion with the body from attacks in ways allowed by the rules. These tend to be reflex reactions on the part of a suddenly frightened opponent.

A competitor's mood for combat can be highly influenced by an advantageous or disadvantageous rate of hitting, loss of self-confidence, or momentary doubt and hesitation. Changes in the psychological background, imaginary or real discontent, the events of the previous days, or unprocessed personal problems can frequently leave marks even in the performance of the best competitors.

Once on the strip, the fencer's thoughts cannot be occupied to the slightest degree with the fact of a disadvantageous pool or draw, the changing circumstances of the competition, the successes of his rivals, the anomalies of the referees, the audience's support for an opponent, one's knowledge of the opponent's superiority, or above average fatigue from previous bouts.

Sustained failures can be forgotten by the reorganization of tactics.

The themes of tactical exercises done in pairs can be:

- Fencing started from an equal score
- Fencing with the fencer's lead
- Fencing with the opponent leading
- Fencing for a single touch to decide the bout
- Fencing in the last minute, or seconds, of the bout
- Fencing for two out of three victories
- Fencing on one or the other side of the strip
- Fencing on the warning line or on the back line
- Fencing without the possibility of retreating
- Only counting touches from attacks or parry ripostes
- The defender can use only simple, or only circle parries
- The ripostes must always be with opposition or flanconades
- The parry is valid only if done in place – or only with breaking the distance.

The coach gives the exercises in the beginning, roughly outlining the possible solutions as well.

VII. Fencing Gymnastics, Exercises, and Games

Training theory unites all of the exercises that adequately develop the necessary abilities under the name of "special preparatory exercises". The following can be initiated and partially achieved:

- Introduction to the requirements
- Adjustment to the sport
- Facing students with their own abilities
- Befriending success and failure
- Developing special abilities, without having a prior knowledge of technique
- Rudiments of tactics
- A partial warm-up

The above-mentioned aims can be approached on a lower level by the use of simple gymnastic exercises, forming them to resemble fencing. The applied method, or form is the evidence of the coach's imagination and his ability to create exercises. We can change

- The order of the movements
- The amplitude
- The frequency
- We can split the symmetry.
- We can make our students symbolically enact periodical and phase-like characteristics of bouts, by breaking continuity, with the use of longer-shorter pauses.

A few examples for illustration:

❖ Hopping in basic position (arms at sides) and in varied sized straddle, one after the other. (1)

❖ Continuous hopping from closed stance to side straddle and back, swinging the arms to shoulder height on landing, changing the size and speed of the straddle, and the length of the pauses that can be incorporated at given points at various times. (2)

❖ Hopping, switching between closed stance and a straddle with arms swung to shoulder height. Switching arms, based on individual decision or the coach's sign, given at random intervals, hopping into closed stance and swinging the arms to shoulder height, while swinging the arm to the side of the body, while hopping to a straddle. The exercise can be played with pairs by dictating and following roles. The follower must repeat the movements of the leader without any delay. (3)

❖ Hopping and switching between basic position and straddle, while sometimes the hands have to be swung to shoulder height at the same time as hopping into straddle and other times raised to shoulder height during the time of two straddle hops. (4)

❖ Hopping into straddle from basic position, then back to basic position while swinging the left arm to shoulder height. Hoping into basic position while swinging the right arm to shoulder height. Hopping into straddle. Hopping into the beginning position while swinging the arms. (5)

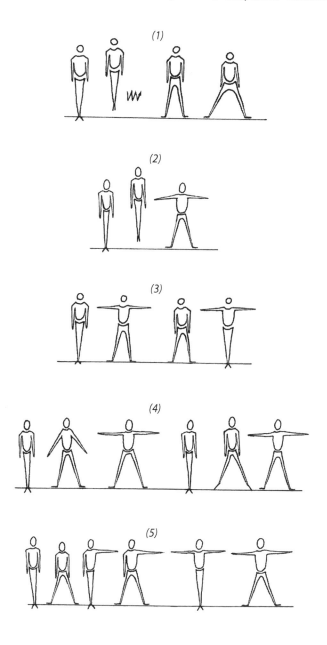

❖ Hopping from basic position to straddle, while swinging the left arm to shoulder height. Hopping into basic position, while swinging the right arm into shoulder height. Hopping into straddle, while swinging the left arm overhead. Hopping into basic position, while swinging the right arm overhead. Hopping into straddle, while swinging the arms to shoulder height. Hopping into the beginning position. (6)

❖ Hopping from basic position to a straddle, while swinging the left arm to shoulder height. Hopping into basic position, while swinging the right arm to shoulder height. Hopping into straddle, while swinging the left arm overhead. Hopping into basic position, while swinging the right arm overhead. Hopping into straddle, while swinging the left arm to shoulder height. Hopping into basic position, while swinging the right arm to shoulder height. Hopping into straddle, while swinging the left arm to the side of the body. Hopping into the beginning position, while letting down the right arm by one's side. (7)

❖ Hopping from basic position to a straddle, while swinging the right arm to shoulder height. Hopping into basic position. Hopping into a straddle, while swinging the left arm to shoulder height. Hopping into basic position, while swinging the left arm overhead. Hopping into the starting position by swinging the arms in the opposite way as well. (8)

❖ Hopping from basic position into a straddle by swinging the right arm to shoulder height and swinging the left arm overhead. Hopping back into the starting position. In the opposite way (left arm to shoulder height, right arm overhead) as well. (9)

(6)

(7)

(8)

(9)

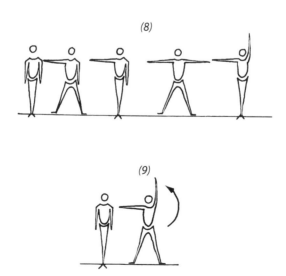

❖ Hopping from basic position into crossways straddle by swinging the arms shoulder height or overhead through shoulder height. Hopping into the starting position. In the opposite way as well.

The above mentioned exercises, especially for beginners, (their place is in the main part of the training practice) refer to the sport's essence (the acyclical and asymmetrical traits), even though they have simple structures. At the same time they also present the students with tools necessary for success, such as the fast redirection of movements or the nature of the ability to quickly change roles.

Although some of the variations allow for steady execution, it is better to avoid the use of command, relying on the ability of the students to solve the problem and struggle along the path to success.

With time, every exercise loses its novelty and the attention necessary for successful execution begins to decrease in direct ratio. As soon as we see this, we should change something about the method of doing the exercise or of its introduction, so the necessary concentration will be achieved again. This can also extend the limits of physical-mental fatigue.

We should take into consideration the age and the mental-physical development of the students when using the exercises, and we should follow the law of gradation.

In the past, future competitors started fencing between the ages of 14-15. Now they begin at 8 – 10. The new starting presents fencing coaches with new challenges. They have to build physical foundations for the youngest parallel to their strictly professional work (that is, not during separate training sessions); at the same time, they have to continue the already initiated development of fencing abilities as long as the age of the students allows this.

(The phrase, "fencing's complementary sport is fencing", which has become a classic, referred – and still refers – to already successful older competitors. For these fencers, movements that differ from those of fencing only meant – and still means – a relaxation from the toils of the sport.)

With the goal of supplementing the missing physical foundations and with expanding the already existing ones:

- The danger of injuries can be decreased by making the muscles and joints stronger and more resistant.
- The reserves of abilities latent in a fencer can be brought to the surface.
- The general workload can be enhanced.
- The disadvantages due to the asymmetrical (one-sided) physical development characteristic of fencing can be decreased.
- At the same time the number of drop-outs can be decreased. The number of those who leave fencing early for one reason or is not low in the younger age groups.

The products of the changing age mentioned above and the exercises on the pages that follow can help in reaching our aims.

❖ Straddle, while the arms are behind and to the sides of the body, with the palms facing backward. Swing the arms at the same time forward through shoulder height and then out to the sides, rotating the hands outwards and upwards into a supinated position and then back to pronation, doing the same route back to the starting position. Repeat. (10)

❖ In a small straddle alternately swing the arms out and back rotating the palms. (11)

❖ Small straddle, arms at shoulder height extended forward. Lower the left and then the right arm to the side of the body with quick rotations of the palms and then raising the arms into the starting position. (12)

❖ Straddle with palms facing upwards with arms stretched to the sides. Lower the arms by bending the elbows (the elbow should stop a span in front of the hip; the forearm should face upwards slightly diagonally). Raise the arms and stretch them into the starting position. (13)

❖ Straddle, arms curved overhead. Swing the arms downward into a sideways diagonal position, then back to the starting position. (14)

❖ From an on guard position with straight legs, extend the weapon arm, swing the non-weapon arm into a "lunge" position, bend the weapon arm back into the on guard position, then swing the non-weapon arm into the on guard position. Repeat continuously. (15)

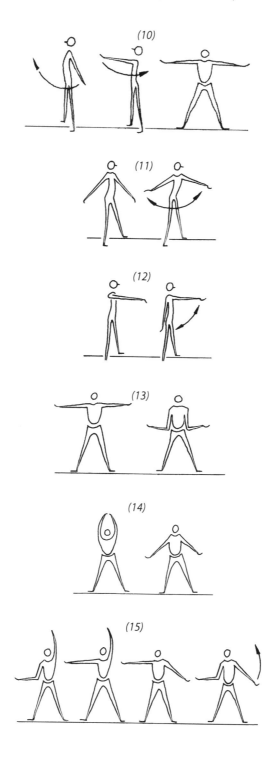

❖ Straddle with parallel feet, palms facing upwards with arms at shoulder height. Slightly open the arms to the sides by slightly bending the elbows, then return to the starting position, Repeat continuously. (16)

❖ The two hands are in front of the chest with bent arms, fingers facing upwards, and palms leaning at each other. Turning the forearm towards the chest inside and outside. (17)

❖ With hands clasped in front of the chest, arms bent (the palm should be facing the chest). Rotate the forearms by stretching the elbows at shoulder height (the palm should be facing forward), then rotate the forearms and bend the elbows back to the starting position. (18)

❖ With hands clasped in front of the body, arms lowered, rotate the palms outward and lift the arms overhead; then rotate the palms and lower the arms into starting position. (19)

❖ With hands clasped overhead, arms extended and palms down, rotate the palms up by bending and stretching the arms at the elbows. (20)

❖ With hands clasped overhead, switch between palms up and down, while repeatedly pulling the arms backward. (21)

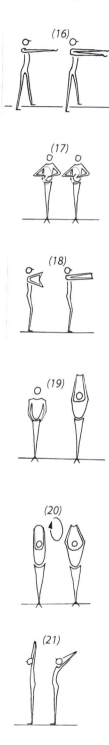

❖ Clasp the hands low behind the body in basic position. Bend the torso forward 2 – 3 times, lifting the arms diagonally overhead, then repeat it with the right leg stepping into an on guard position with extended legs. In the opposite way as well. (22)

❖ Clasp the hands behind the body straddle-legged. Slowly bend the torso forward, while lifting the arms into a rear diagonal overhead position, then raise the body and lower the arms into the starting position. (23)

❖ From a straddle, knees straight, bend the torso forward, switching between the left and right palm, fingers touching the outer part of the left and the right ankle. (24)

❖ In lunge position, clasp the hands behind the body. Slowly bend the torso forward, while lifting the arms into a rear diagonal overhead position, then lower the arms back into the starting position while stretching the torso. (25)

❖ Lunge position, hands overhead. Rotate the torso to the right and backward in the direction of the extended leg. The opposite way as well. (26)

❖ From a right or left-handed on guard, bend the torso forward and touch the ground while straightening the knees. (27)

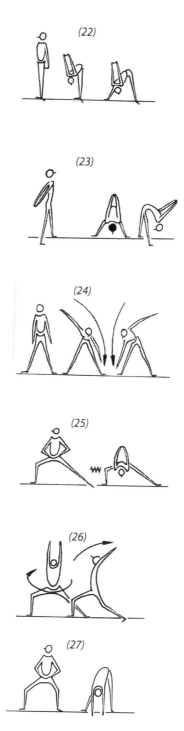

(22)

(23)

(24)

(25)

(26)

(27)

❖ Seated on the floor, straddle with the left sole against the right thigh (often called "figure 4 position"). Bend the torso forward in the direction of the extended leg, while switching between tightened and pointing foot positions. The opposite way as well. (28)

❖ Sit with legs straight and feet pointing upward, hands behind the body. Bend the torso continuously, touching the ankle and the foot with both hands, while rotating the outer sides of the feet against the ground. (29)

❖ Kneeling with legs apart and the inside of both ankles touching the floor, slowly sit down and lie back between the splayed legs, then return to beginning position *(Editor's caution: this places considerable strain on the knees)*. (30)

❖ With toes pointed up, lie supine on the floor with straddled legs. The two arms are extended approximately to the sides, while the palms are on the floor. Raise the back off the floor and place the outside part of the ankles on the floor, while the toes are pointing sideways, and then back to the beginning position. (31)

❖ Bend your torso forward quickly in a small straddle. Raise your toes and touch them, then return to the beginning position. (32)

❖ In a closed stance or in a straddle, keep alternating between heels in the air (standing on your toes) and toes in the air (standing on your heels). (33)

(28)

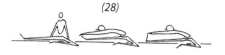

(29)

(30)

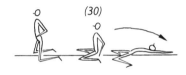

(31)

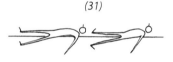

(32)

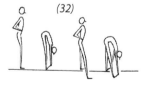

(33)

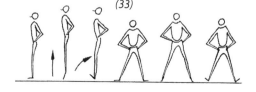

❖ Lie on your stomach with the legs in a small straddle with hands under the shoulders. Lift the torso with a half push-up and press your heels to the floor, then back to the beginning position. (34)

❖ Sit with your hands touching the floor behind your body and your legs lifted in a straddle. Make circles with your feet inside and outside. Change between pointing your toes and pointing your heels. (35)

❖ Stand on your toes in a straddle and rotate both of your ankles in the same or opposite direction, starting inside or outside. (36)

❖ Stand on your toes in an on guard position with straight legs, then bend your knees and sink into on guard. Back to the beginning position by straightening your legs. (37)

❖ Bounce a couple of times in a normal on guard, then a couple of times in a wider, deeper on guard. (38)

❖ From on guard, lift yourself up onto your toes; extend your knees, then immediately back to the beginning position (or have a slight pause while standing on your toes). (39)

(34)

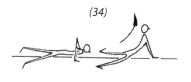

(35)

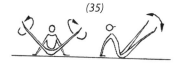

(36)

(37)

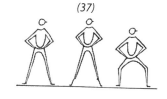

(38)

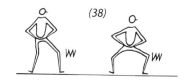

(39)

187

❖ Stretch the Achilles' tendon by leaning against the bars or the wall. (40)

❖ Moving the feet as shown in the figure while sitting on a stool or a bench. (41)

❖ Lift your heels alternately in on guard position. (42)

❖ Stand on one leg. Extend the other leg and swing it back and forth, either with toes straightened or pointing upward. Then change. (43)

❖ In a squat position, with the arms extended forward at shoulder height, slowly stand up on tiptoes (still squatting); then sink back to the beginning position. (44)

❖ March in place in on guard position, simply by lifting and placing the feet on the floor, one after the other. (45)

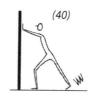

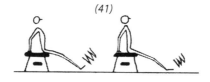

❖ Bounce in a squat position, switching between closed and open knees – in place or back and forth. (46)

❖ Jump up from one foot and cross your legs in the air after two or three steps forward. Land on the floor with two feet. (47)

❖ Jump in the air, after two or three steps forward, from the right and then the left foot and have the ankles touch each other. Land on both feet. (48)

❖ Sit on the floor in an extended straddle, while the arms are extended at shoulder height. Lift the two legs at the same time and clap your feet together. (49)

❖ Stand in on guard or in a straddle slantwise with slightly bent knees. Place a tennis ball on the opened fingers of the right hand. When the attention is at its height, pull the hand out under the ball and catch it with a movement going from up to down, before it hits the floor. (The second half of the movement should be faster.) The smaller circle we make around the ball, the less it will lose from its original height. (50)

❖ Do the same as in the previous exercise, and do one or two claps on the left hand or the right thigh before catching the ball. (51)

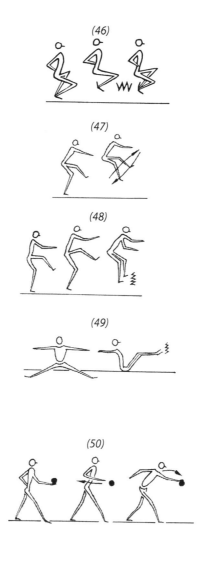

(46)

(47)

(48)

(49)

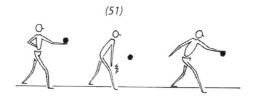

(50)

(51)

❖ Do the same as in the previous exercise, and do one clap on the left hand and one on the right thigh. (52)

❖ Do the same as in the previous exercise, but reverse the order of the claps. (53)

❖ Stand in a straddle with bent knees or in on guard. Throw a tennis ball on the floor and catch it in a running motion where the legs cross each other or in a fleche, when the ball is lifting off from the floor. (54)

❖ From on guard, catch the glove thrown forward by a partner with a fleche. (55)

❖ Standing in a straddle, roll a basketball, volleyball, etc., around the body, around the shoulders, and around the legs, using the coordinated work of the fingers and the wrist. (56)

❖ Holding a basketball or volleyball, stand in a medium or large on guard in front of a wall. The weapon hand should be behind the ball with fingers facing upwards in the beginning and at the end of the exercise, while the weaponless hand should be touching the ball from the inside.

　　Throw the ball against the wall. When throwing it, take a step forward in on guard position and use the strong, pushing movement of the weapon arm to push away the

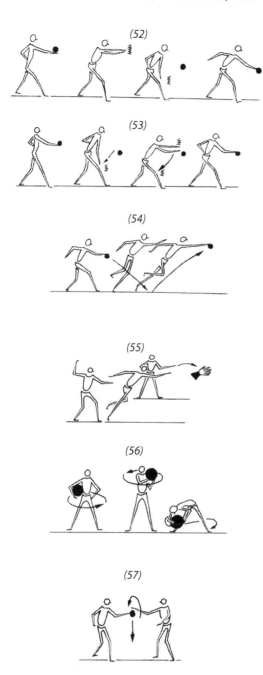

ball. As the ball bounces off the wall, escort it back by bending the weapon arm, taking up the on guard position again, or taking a step backward as well, to reestablish the size of the large on guard position.

❖ Like the previous exercise, but now before touching the returning ball, do one or two claps with both hands. Footwork can be sped up with the faster back and forth pushing movement of the weapon hand.

❖ The above-mentioned exercise in pairs, passing the ball with lunges or step lunges.

❖ Moving the ball in an on guard position on the weapon hand side of the body, in place, marching in place, or keeping an imaginary distance with back and forth steps, sometimes imitating the attacker's role with a lunge, or step forward.

❖ Like the above-mentioned exercise, but in pairs this time, adjust to the roles of the attackers and defenders. One person of the pair (the leader), standing in on guard, should hold a tennis ball in his palm, while the palm is facing downwards. The partner should place his hand on or above his partner's hand, with his palm facing downwards or the thumb facing upwards. The leader should try to let go of the ball as inconspicuously as possible, and the pair should try to catch the ball as soon as possible, with a motion similar to the use of a spoon. (57) Practice can be made more realistic, from a fencer's aspect, by creating distracting moments with the hand, the arm, with sounds, feinting, marching on spot, or with the use of fencing steps. The chances of success are increased by taking advantage of the impulses resulting from peripheral vision and the sense of touch.

❖ Like the previous exercise, but with two balls, standing with knees bent in a straddle sideways. The balls can be let go separately (in such instances, only the competent hand, arm is allowed to react) or at the same time. The exercise can be more difficult if one or both of the partners are marching in place.

❖ The same exercise as before, but each of the partners holds one ball. The assignment is double: the "fencer" can be two-in-one, the leader and the adjuster, the attacker and the defender.

❖ Another partner drill: One person, standing in a straddle with bent knees, should raise both of his arms, palms facing each other, to a horizontal line with his own body. The person facing him should try to move his weapon hand between the partner's palms, up and down, then down and up. The person standing in the straddle should try and clap his palms to stop the opponent form moving his hand through. (58)

❖ The pair should stand facing each other in a bent straddle slantwise or in on guard and play the familiar game where you have to suddenly slap the opponent's hand with one hand either from palm-to-palm contact (59) or without contact starting from a fixed position. (60)

(58)   *(59)*   *(60)*

❖ Play the hand slapping game with two hands. (61) This can have a variation, when one of the fencer's hands is placed above and the other one is placed under. This way, both sides can be attackers and defenders at the same time. (62)

❖ The fencers should be in pairs, facing each other in a straddle slantwise with bent knees or in on guard. The defender should hold his weapon hand in on guard position with the palm facing upwards. The attacker should try to hit the weapon hand on the palm with a descending movement, imitating the movement of a crossing gate. The defender tries to withdraw his hand.

❖ The same exercise as above, but attacker tries to hit defender's hand with a lunge. Defender can withdraw the hand, retreat, or both. The partners should not stand too far from each. (63)

❖ The same exercise (without the lunge), but now, the attacker must avoid the opponent with a fleche or by running after a successful hit. (64)

❖ One-handed "cock-fighting" while hopping on one foot, trying to push the opponent's hand to unbalance him. The person to place his second foot on the floor will be the loser. (65)

❖ Hold hands in a straddle. Try to move the opponent from his initial position with the use of pushing-pulling movements. (66)

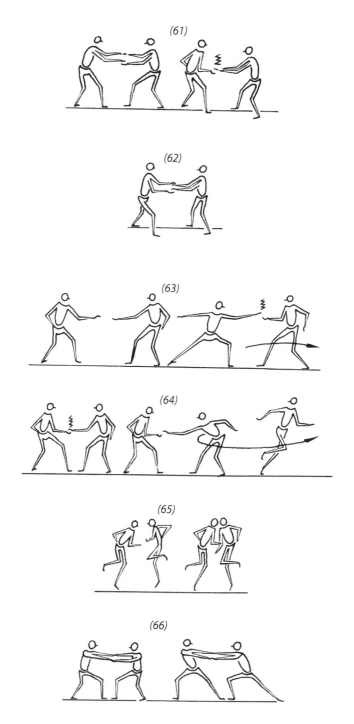

(61)

(62)

(63)

(64)

(65)

(66)

❖ Take up a push-up position. Lift and drop the hips, jump into a squat, and finish with a fleche. (67)

❖ Jump over the partner with a leapfrog jump after a short run-up. (68) The jumper should land

- In an on guard position in the direction of the jump
- Or perpendicular to it in a right or left handed on guard
- Or in a lunge, perpendicular to the direction of the jump (The person should adjust his feet in the air according to the desired landing position.)

Do a fleche when you land in the direction of the jump.

The roles should change after each jump or according to the coach's desire. The exercise can be done throughout the whole fencing hall as a race when landing in the direction of the on guard, jumping continuously and switching after each jump. Experienced fencers in a lower position can provide a larger arc and a longer chance of flying if they lift themselves upwards and diagonally forward in the proper time. Partners should provide for a secure landing at the expected spot for finishing.

❖ Lie on your back with knees pulled up and push your partner forward with an upward movement. After a short flight, partner should land in on guard and fleche, or land in a squat position, return to on guard, and fleche. In order to avoid accidents, the assistance of partners is necessary. (69)

❖ Do a lunge from a fencing basic position in a squat, and then back to the initial position. (70)

(67)

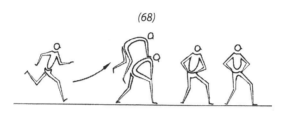

(68)

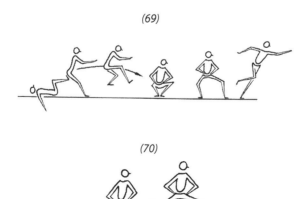

(69)

(70)

❖ Bend your knees while lifting your arms to shoulder height; then return to starting position. (71)

❖ From a lunge, take a step forward with the rear foot into a squatting basic position and then step backward into the initial position. (72)

❖ From a fencing basic position in a squat, move the rear foot backward into a lunge, then close with the front leg back to the beginning position. (73)

❖ From a fencing basic position in a squat, do a lunge and recover forward with your rear leg into the squat position. Repeat. (74)

❖ Squat slowly from a fencing basic position by bending the knees, and then back to beginning position. (75)

❖ From fencing basic position take 2-3 steps always arriving in a larger on guard and then take one step backward into the starting position. (76)

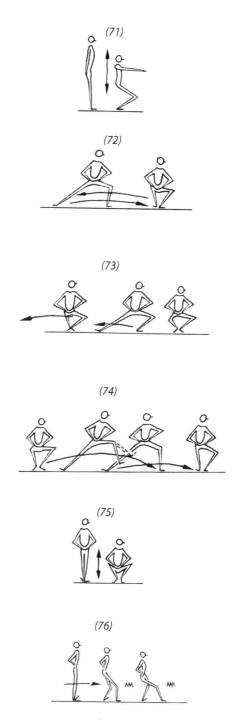

❖ Raise your arms overhead, palms facing each other, in fencing basic position. Step forward into on guard while lowering the right hand to shoulder height. Do a lunge while swinging the non-weapon arm to shoulder height. Take a step backward into on guard and swinging the left hand overhead and finally swing the weapon arm overhead and close the feet arriving back into the starting position. (77)

❖ In a squat position with opened knees, touch the floor. Slowly stretch your knees by keeping the support or by touching the floor with fingertips. (78)

❖ Alternately hop in closed stance, in fencing basic stance, and the fencing stance, adding longer-shorter pauses. (79)

❖ Hopping in fencing basic position, occasionally pulling up the heels. (80)

❖ Start from a kneeling position, situated between a fencing basic position and an on guard, according to the coach's commands: "Ready!" "Steady!" "Go!" After the start, do a few running steps or fleche with legs crossing each other. (81)

(77)

(78)

(79)

(80)

(81)

❖ From a push-up, pull in the hips and jump into a narrow or wide on guard; then do a fleche. (82)

❖ Squat and hop forward a few times and then land in on guard. (83)

❖ Jump up from a basic position, pull up your knees, and land in a basic position with bent knees – or squatting in on guard position – and do a fleche. (84)

❖ Hop on both feet. Do a few claps in front of the body while you are jumping up according to your preferred timing. (85)

❖ Turn the hips right and left while hopping on both feet. (86)

❖ Hop on both feet and jump up a couple of times, doing a clap in front of or behind the body. Sometimes during claps, cross your legs in the air or touch the two ankles to each other. (87)

(82)

(83)

(84)

(85)

(86)

(87)

❖ Hop forward on right or left foot, land in on guard, and then do a fleche. (88)

❖ Jump up while hopping in an on guard position and then cross the legs, do a straddle, pull up the knees, or lift the heels. (89)

❖ Hop in basic position and in on guard position in differing height and speed, changing between the two positions at various intervals. (90)

❖ After hopping forward in on guard, land in a deep on guard position and fleche. (91)

❖ Jump forward from on guard. Using the arms and legs, arrive in a deep on guard; then fleche. Sometimes before the fleche, clap the hand on the floor, or switching the frequency and doing one on the floor and the next one with hands. (92)

(88)

(89)

(90)

(91)

(92)

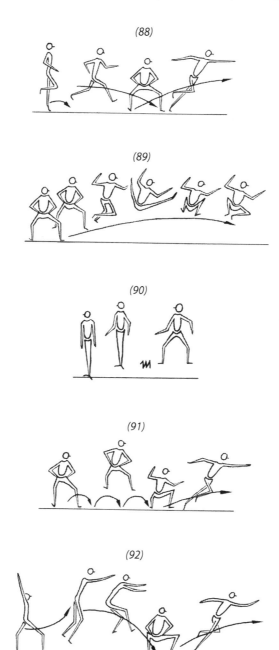

❖ Swinging both your arms energetically, do a jump from a kneeling position where the feet are pushed backward on the floor. Energetically swing the arm and stretch the knees, land in a right or left-handed on guard, then do a fleche. After the jump, the height and depth of the on guard position is in relation to the energy gained by the hand- and legwork. (93)

❖ Lean forward in on guard, touch the floor, then fleche. (94)

❖ Hop from a sideways straddle and land in a right or left attacking position (see figure), sometimes lifting the arms to shoulder height. (95)

❖ Hop on both feet; sometimes jump up and cross the feet or make a scissor-like movement. (96)

❖ From a straddle, do a left and then a right attacking position (see figure) without raising the center of gravity. (97)

(93)

(94)

(95)

(96)

(97)

❖ From basic position, step forward into an attacking position with the right and then the left foot. (98)

❖ From a squatting position, stretch your left leg backward. Holding the position, switch between the feet at random intervals. (99)

❖ From a push-up, pull in the hips and arrive into a right or left-handed squatting on guard position. (100)

❖ Short jumps backward from on guard position while crossing the feet. (101)

❖ After holding a lunge, turn in the direction of the chest into the opposite handed lunge and do a fleche. (102)

❖ Practice the first half of a jump in on guard while standing in on guard and stamping on the floor with the pinned down foot. (103)

(98)

(99)

(100)

(101)

(102)

(103)

❖ From on guard, jump into a squatting position, lunge, then fleche. (104)

❖ From on guard, swing the front foot forward, then back to the on guard; then, starting with the same motion, lunge. (105)

❖ Do knee bends from basic position; jump into on guard, and lunge. (106)

❖ Step forward into on guard from a basic position; close the feet, take a step backward into on guard, close the feet. (107)

❖ From on guard, lift the front foot,, swing it forward, then back to the beginning position. Repeat several times. (108)

❖ In lunge position, push yourself backward by extending the front knee, then forward into lunge position by extending the rear knee. (109)

(104)

(105)

(106)

(107)

(108)

(109)

❖ Do knee bends from on guard and then jump forward and backward with both feet. (110)

❖ Stretch the leg forward in a fencing basic position. Then extend the bent knee and bend the extended leg; turn 180 degrees into the opposite handed beginning position doing it back-and-forth a number of times. (111)

❖ Do a fleche after slightly bending the knees in on guard. (112)

❖ Do 6-8 continuous jumps forward in on guard. (113)

❖ From on guard close the feet with the rear foot into basic position with bent knees, back to beginning position, close with the front foot, back to on guard. (114)

❖ From a push-up position swing the right leg in a circle into a lunge, keeping the hands on the floor, and then back to the beginning position. Do it the opposite way as well. (115)

(110)

(111)

(112)

(113)

(114)

(115)

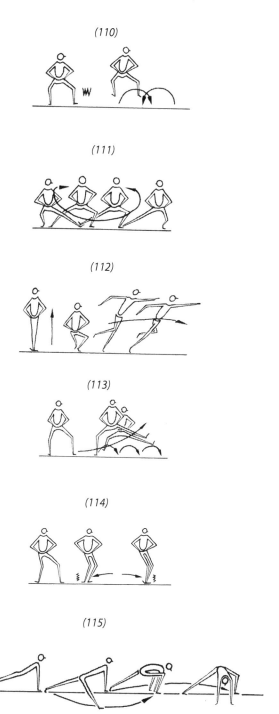

❖ Switching between bouncing in on guard and in lunge position. (116)

❖ Clasp the hands in the fencing basic position. Bend forward, lifting the arms overhead. (117)

❖ From a squatting fencing basic position, stretch the pointing right foot forward. Roll over to a lunge and then back to the starting position. The same thing the opposite way also: that is stretch the pointing left foot sideways from a squatting fencing basic position. Roll over to the beginning position. (118)

❖ Jump up from a fencing basic position and pull up the knees. (119)

❖ Jump up and lift the heels while bouncing in a fencing basic position. (120)

(116)

(117)

(118)

(119)

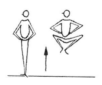

(120)

❖ Do a jump from a kneeling position, where the feet are pushed backward on the floor and swing both your arms into a squatting basic position; then do a fleche. Do this from both right- and left-handed squatting positions. (121)

❖ Roll back from a lunge into a squatting basic position by bending the extended leg; roll over to the beginning position and do a fleche. (122)

❖ From on guard, do a cross-step backward placing the front foot behind the rear heel, bending the knees deeper; then go back to the starting position. The opposite way as well. (123)

❖ Stand on your left leg and hold your right foot with your left hand. Jump forward over the right leg. (124)

❖ Lower yourself from a fencing basic position into a bent basic position, by sliding the right leg forward with an extended knee, and then push yourself back up into the starting position. (125)

(121)

(122)

(123)

(124)

(125)

❖ Skip in fencing basic position. (126)

❖ Squat from fencing basic position, lifting the arms to shoulder height. Then bend your body forward, touching the ground with your hands while straightening the knees. (127)

❖ Swing the right leg forward-and-back, high, from the fencing basic position, close the legs, swing the left leg back-and-forth, high, and close the legs. (128)

❖ From the push-up position, supporting your body with both hands, continuously jump into right- and left-handed lunges.

❖ The same exercise as above, but do not support with your hands and bring your body to a vertical position when landing in the lunge. The movements should follow each other without pauses. The coach should decide the frequency.

❖ While running in place, do an on guard or a lunge based on the coach's signal.

❖ Partner drill: One member of the pair, the helper, should stand behind his partner, who is in a lunge position. The helper should lift his partner's ankle and raise it to approximately the height of the bent knee in a lunge. After this the person doing the lunge should do some knee

(126)

(127)

(128)

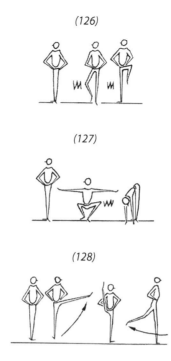

stretches, knee bends, and finally a few small hops forward with the help of the assisting partner and based on his commands.

* Like the previous exercise, but now the partner lifting the ankle should slightly pull the extended leg horizontally backward (the lunge will be pulled in the direction of a split because of this, the bent leg should stay in its position), then push it back to the original position. After doing it a few times, switch roles.

* Pairs, with their backs touching, sit in straddle with extended legs and their hands holding each other's extended overhead. One person should slowly bend his body and pull the other person on himself, and then he should release him back into the starting position, doing this a number of times.

❖ One person stands in a lunge and raises both of his hands overhead. The partner, standing behind him, should hold the hands or wrists and with intensive physical assistance, he should help the person sit in a hurdling position by turning 180 degrees towards the chest, and then help him stand up in a similar method and route going back to the beginning position.

❖ Pairs stand with their backs to each other with their elbows clasped. On the command, they sit on the floor simultaneously, then stand up simultaneously, solely by pressing their backs to other and using their legs, either resisting with them when sitting down or pushing with them, when standing up. At an advanced level, a leg of one or both partners can be lifted in the air and keeping it there, to place more strain on the working leg. The exercise can be done by switching between the legs while doing it.

❖ The partners should stand in guard position, facing the same direction, with their backs to each other and clasp their elbows. (One of the fencers will be in a right-handed on guard, the other in a left-handed on guard, regardless of what their original hand is.) They should take small steps and do lunges according to the given signal, always working in concert with each other. When doing the lunge, the two arms have to be swung to shoulder height. It will be harder to move in concert when the partners can only make contact by pressing their backs to each other. In such instances, the students should hold and use their arms like fencers do. (The coach should not forget about switching.)

❖ Pairs should stand with their backs to each other, either clasping their elbows or holding hands overhead. One person should bend his knees, shifting the line of his shoulders beneath the partner's shoulder blades or close to it; then he should hunch down and lift his partner on his back, do some suspensions, and bend the knees a few times. The person lifted on the back is dangling his legs, while being positioned in a semi-circle position.

Game possibilities in fencing halls.

Due to their tensionless atmosphere, games should mainly or strictly be in the last, finishing phases of training sessions and the coach should only use these as beginning exercises on rare occasions, aware of the risk that it will become more difficult to get the students to do technical work.

1. The space for playing should be big enough for the person who is tagged to change quickly. The tagged person ("It") should raise his left hand and say his first name loudly, while running, or the opposite way around, raise his right hand and say his last name, in order to signal his momentary status. The coach can dictate "change" in case of advanced students, to make their jobs more difficult. The game requires greater mental discipline in this case.

2. Place benches in the four corners of the designated playing field, and one shorter bench in the middle. (The benches in the corners should cut off space, but there should be enough room for people to run behind them.) One player is designated the chaser. Students who are being chased can jump over the benches; the chaser can only go around them. Players who are caught must leave the playing field. The total game time should be quite short (maximum 2-3 minutes), so the students will be forced to move and to orientate themselves fast. At the end of the game, the person with the most catches is the winner.

3. The fencers should pick up their partners on their backs. The coach should appoint the chaser pair. Only the "rider" can tag others. (When being tagged, one cannot tag the previous chaser!) It is worth playing the game on a narrow area.

   Older fencers, adults, can play the game by switching the roles. The coach should initiate the change while the players are in motion: the "horse" becomes the "rider" and vice versa. There should not be a long pause during the change.

4. The coach should arrange the students into two rows facing each other with equal numbers. (The fencers will be competing in pairs.) There should be larger room between beginners and children and smaller room between advanced fencers and competition fencers. (Distance can be decreased step by step as the game progresses.) One row will be "black", the other "white". The row, decided by the coach, should run or do a fleche while trying to catch the members of the opposite row by hitting their hands within 2-3 steps. If the students start their movements by stretching their weapon arms, they will have greater chances in hitting on a short distance. (Implicitly, the fleche must be started by stretching the hand and the arm.)

   The start can happen from a slantwise or a sideways straddle, in on guard with bent or extended knees, stepping in place in an on guard position, while jumping on spot or back-and-forth, or from a lunge. The rows can be facing each other or they can have their backs to each other; they can start from similar or different positions.

   The strain of advanced and competition fencers can be increased with short pauses during continuous starts. Students in this case should hurry up when taking up their starting positions, so they can avoid hearing the coach's command while still being in motion.

The row called upon by the coach should be the chaser in the beginning, the other row the one who is fleeing, later the other way around, the called upon row will flee and the other one will be chasing.

The coach can make the job difficult for those who gain experience, by giving the "switch" command while the players are in motion. This way the task of the rows can be changed a number of times, without stopping the game.

5. ("Steal the Bacon") The coach should place a glove on a mask turned sideways in the middle of two rows facing each other. Students standing in the rows should be labeled with numbers. The smallest number of one row should be facing the largest number from the other row. For example, if there are eight people in a row, number eight of one row should be facing number one of the other row, number seven should be facing number two and so on.

The coach should call out a number. People labeled with the number should run and try to get the glove and take it behind their own row or they should stop the opponent from doing so, by tagging the person who has taken the glove. (Thus the exercise has two goals, so no one can concentrate on one thing only.) The team who succeeds in the exercise gets the point. Each game should go on for a set time or an announced amount of points.

The distance between the rows should be as big as the distance that will be between the future fencers when they start bouts or when they take up the on guard after successful hits.

The rows can start by facing each other or their backs facing each other, from on guard or from a lunge, stepping in place in on guard, hopping in place, or changing between the positions of on guard and lunge with flat jumps. The start position can be the same or different for each row.

The necessary advantage in cadence can be achieved by the use of the hand, arm and (or) moving on one's own side of the field.

6. ("Musical Chairs") Place items suitable for sitting, one minus the number of students, in a big circle around the fencing hall (a chair, stool, or medicine ball). Students should start running outside of the circle, and then based on the coach's signal they should try and find an item around them to quickly sit on. The person who cannot sit down gets a hit.

7. (Dodgeball) The coach should choose a student who has to hit the other with a rubber ball inside a set area. The student should try to hit as many as the coach decides within a given time. (You cannot give a valid hit if the ball hit someone by bouncing off the floor.) Each hit is worth one point; the thrower counts the points. People who are hit should sit down immediately, so it is obvious who is still in play. At the end of the game, the order can be set up according to the points collected.

8. Dodgeball with two balls. The coach should bring the balls into play. There is no one determined to be the thrower in this version; everyone can be it, if they manage to get the ball. (Everyone counts his or her own points.) Balls bouncing off the floor do not count as points, just as if someone catches a ball in the air that was thrown at him. The coach should announce the winner at the end of the game.

9. Paired dodge ball. The members of the pairs can assist each other. The person with the ball can pass it to the partner, who meanwhile has time to find a better place to hit someone successfully. If a member of a pair is hit, he should sit down immediately; he cannot hit anyone from then on. However, if he is able to catch the ball in the air, thrown by his pair, or pick up the ball from the floor, then he can reenter the game.

10. The coach should set up the students in a circle,

where they are tightly next to each other in a small straddle. They should look forward to the middle of the circle, while their body is slightly bent forward and their hands are resting on their lower backs, between their hipbones. The coach (or an appointed student) should move slowly or fast, sometimes changing the direction and place the glove he is holding in the hands of a student who is standing in the circle. The student who gets the glove should chase the person on his right or left (decided by the coach) for one round, while he hits – gently! – the fleeing person on his back, under the sacrum and the line of the waist as many times as he can. Once the chased person is back to his original position, the game starts again.

11. Students should stand in front of the coach in a single line, standing in on guard. (Lefties should be at the end of the line to their left.) The coach should give commands such as "forward!" or "backward!" and the students should act accordingly. Those who hesitate, who are late, or the ones who switch the directions should sit out. Those who are in the game until its end will decide the fate of the game.

12. It will be more difficult to do it without mistakes if the students have to react in the opposite way to the frequency as well and not only the direction (this time, "One!" stands for two and "Two!" stands for one step.)

13. For fencers who have "smelled gunpowder", the gradual decease in space (the closer fencers get to each other, the more difficult it will be to overcome the instincts and not to copy the neighbor who makes a mistake) and the quick changes in the commands allow tension to increase.

14. The coach should line up his students in front of a wall (8 – 10 meters from it) in a single line with the commands, "On guard!", "Ready!". (The beginning position can face the wall or facing it with the back in on

guard, lunge, squat,, lying on the stomach or the back, in a normal push-up or a push-up on the back, sitting with crossed legs, or the standing or kneeling start of athletics.) Once students hear "Go!", they should run up to the wall, and clap on it with their weapon hand 2-3 times (by stretching the arm or doing a lunge). Following this, they should turn and run back behind the starting line as fast as they can to take up their original starting position. The coach should decide on the first, second, and third places, in case the crowd is big, a student should help him. Starting the group and announcing the results can only happen when everyone is either standing or sitting motionless behind the line.

15. (Relays) Students should stand in 2-3 rows, depending on their head count. The first students of the rows should run, hop on their right or left feet, or do fencing steps forward or backward. They should go around the medicine ball, stool, or mask, placed 8 – 10 meters in front of their row, and afterwards they should clap their partner's hand, so the next person can take his turn. The starting position should be in on guard or a standing start position. Starting someone's turn and switching turns can only happen behind the line. The last students from the rows and their time of arrival decide the competition. The coach can change the method of execution, the direction of the turns, their frequency, between rounds. A person in a team with uneven numbers should go twice; he should start and finish the game.

16. ("Suicides") Students should line up next to each other in a single line on the strip's rear line. Following the signal, they should start running, touch the strip's center line 2-3 times, run back to the rear line, which they touch 2-3 times, then run and touch the far warning line and back to the finish line and they take up the position they were in before the start. One can announce results based on the first three (in case

there are a lot of people, only the first person), who finishes first and takes up his original position. The person doing a small lunge, to approach the lines and do the touches, can reduce the times of completing the distances. He saves time and space by this for the following laps.

17. Position the students in 2 lines in 2 diagonally opposite corners of the fencing hall. (The distance between the fencers should be more than 2 – 3 meters.) One person from a pair, following the line of the diagonal, tries to mislead the other person who is attempting to copy him, by running fast, slow, stopping suddenly, or changing the direction abruptly. Once a pair does the exercise, they should line up behind those who are getting ready, so the whole exercise will be continuous. The pairs should tightly follow each other.

18. Place three jumping stools, 1 meter apart from each other, in front of our students standing in a row, while a fourth stool should be placed 1.5 – 2 meters and the fifth on 1 meter again. (The distance between the stools depends on the students' age (body height) and their fencing skills, if necessary, it can be modified, in given instances the stools can be changed to fencing masks.) Students in the row should hop on their right or left feet through the first three stools, tightly following each other, they should arrive in on guard on the larger space between the third and the fourth stool, the should jump over the fifth stool with one foot to arrive in on guard, then they should immediately do a fleche. Once they are done, they should line up again straight away, so the practice will be continuous.

19. Students should line up in a single row and run through a jump rope, swung by two students standing in front of the row, continuously, following each other, or by leaving out two-three cadences, without letting the jump rope touch them. (129) (The direction of the swinging should go from top to bottom, when

viewing it from the position of the students' point of view.) The single swing of the rope gives the timing of the exercise. The length of the rope, the distance between the people swinging the rope, the speed of swinging it, and the distance between the rope and the starting position should be changed according to the students' abilities (their reaction time, their abilities to start the exercise, the speed of their movements.)

The exercise can start from on guard, stepping in place in on guard, stepping back and forth, or jump-

(129)

ing in place. Running or fleche should be used to pass through the rope. Pairs can also execute the exercise. In such cases, a member of the pair gives a verbal, or motioning starting signal. The partner, playing the role of an opponent has a more difficult job, when tricks are used during the exercise. The students swinging the rope can stop suddenly, while changing their position, and the increase and decrease in distance, urges the students, preparing to attempt the exercise, to maintain the ideal distance.

More jump ropes can be swung at the same time with proper distance between them. The fencers should pass through the ropes either continuously, or with stops, halting in front of some of the ropes. They should either wait still or they should move, while preparing for the next sign of a tempo. Students with enough experience in the game can do a few jumps under the rope, before running out or doing the fleche.

20. One member of a pair should squeeze a rubber- or volleyball between his ankles in a sitting position and the partner should stand next to him in the line of the ball. The person with the ball should lie on the floor with his back and he should throw the ball behind himself as far as he can, so the ball flies on an arch-like path. The partner should retrieve the ball and place it between the ankles. The game, the competition between the members of a pair should go on for a limited time or up to a limited number of points.

21. Two fencers stand in front of each other at a close distance, ready to start, with bent knees in a crossways or sideways straddle. The "attacker" holds a ball, which he should release, roll, or throw, forward or backward above his own head or above the partner's head. The "attacker" can be still or he can move, he can use feints or direct movements. The "attacked" person should try and reach the ball and put it back into the partner's hands. The exercise is to discover the feints and to maintain speed.

22. Indoor soccer can be played by setting up the goals 1-1.5 meters from the walls, instead of placing them strictly by the side of the walls. (The game thus becomes similar to hockey, since it will be played behind the goals as well.) Goals can be worth two points in this game. The coach or the student leading the game can change the 3-4 member teams in the middle of matches, according to the changes of the games. In given instances, some of the players can be switched.

Bibliography

1. Gusztáv Tomanóczy – Alfréd Gellér: A vívás kézikönyve, 1942 (The handbook of fencing)
2. Dr. Laszló Duronelly: Vívás, TF. Jegyzet, 1951, 1962 (Fencing, TF. Notes)
3. Dr. Béla Bay – Dr. Béla Rerrich – Endre Tilli: Tőr és párbajtőrvívás, 1953 (Foil and epee fencing)
4. Dr. László Duronelly: A vívás alapelemei és oktatása, 1954 (Basic elements and education of fencing)
5. Dr. Béla Rerrich – Endre Tilli: A magyar vívás kézikönyve, 1954 (The handbook of Hungarian fencing)
6. László Szabó: A vívás és oktatása, 1971 (Fencing and its education) Published in English as *Fencing and the Master*, SKA SwordPlay Books
7. Dr. Robert Duronelly – István Lukovich: Vívás, 1975 (Fencing)

Made in the USA
San Bernardino, CA
23 June 2016